PARKINSON'S:
With Purpose

PARKINSON'S: With Purpose

My Path Through Pain

John K Williams

ISBN: 979-8-3369-8828-4

Cover design and photo by: John K Williams
Colombia River Park

DEDICATION

PASTOR CURT (PC) SEABURG

It was his encouragement to me to write a book using stories from my journal of how God used me while dealing with Parkinson's. At some point in my illness, I decided that writing a book wasn't worth the effort and I couldn't see why anyone would read it. Then came the day that PC told one of my stories to the congregation. At one point in his message he said, "John, you've got to write a book." That was it. I had to write this book.

CONTENTS

FORWARD

Parkinson's: With Purpose is my personal story based on my struggle with Parkinson's Disease. I have been asking God, "Why me?" I have been dealing with all the issues that accompany PD, wrestling with questions and my purpose in life. After diagnosis, I spent the next six months solely trying to figure out the disease, only to find a myriad of symptoms. If you were diagnosed with Parkinson's, the factors that contribute to your symptoms are unique to you and will probably be different from others.

While you are looking for answers, I encourage you to live out your unfulfilled dreams. I once heard someone say, there is an unfulfilled assignment with your name on it. Parkinson's can be a new lease on life if you stay active and search for your purpose. Get your eyes off your illness and onto what God is doing. Allow this season in your life to build character, as you focus on others.

Join me on my journey. At times it is not pretty. Watch how God unravels my thoughts and reveals His plan and purpose for my life while dealing with Parkinson's. I pray that you find ways to implement strategies into your life. Daily, I'm learning how to surrender my plans and accept what God has orchestrated in my life to further His kingdom. Not my will, but God's will be done. What started as a death sentence, in my mind, became an adventure in ways I hadn't dreamed possible.

Although this book is intended for people with Parkinson's and other disabilities, my prayer is that everyone may benefit from it. Challenges in life are not limited to people with medical conditions.

No matter how much you lack, it is enough in the hands of Jesus. The fishes and loaves were not enough, except in the hands of the Master. But the real miracle took place as the disciples obeyed and distributed among the people. As I surrender my life, finances, and possessions to God, it becomes more than enough in His hands. I just need to distribute in obedience.

God stretches me and takes me to levels that I never expect. The people surrounding my ministry are so important! I tell stories several times in this book that show this principle. It's not just about you! Sometimes we need our eyes opened to what God is doing, so we stop focusing on ourselves. This is my story of how God opened my eyes.

DISCLAIMER:

Please do not interpret anything I say as medical advice. It is just information about the things that I have done that helps me. It is always important to check with your health care provider before making any changes to your health care program.

ACKNOWLEDGEMENTS,
Special thanks to:

God, the Father, who created me with purpose.

Jesus, the Son, who forgives me and gives me new life, who carries me when I struggle, and then sets me down with my feet headed in the right direction.

Holy Spirit, who gives me instructions towards my adventures and then gives me boldness to carry out the plan.

My wife, Karen, for her time and dedication in helping me complete this book.

All who continue to pray for me, as I battle with Parkinson's. And to all who share in my journey as I become salt and light in a fallen world.

Thank you, Amy, Dawnell, and Thelma, for sharing your experiences in writing your books.

Thanks to Margaret High for editing the text.

Thanks to the unsung heroes of Parkinson's disease, the caretakers! What you contribute is beyond the call of duty. Your sacrifice surpasses that which cannot be measured. Your reward will be great.

Bobbi, Devon, Jodi, Kathleen, Kristy, Leah, Linda, Marci, Maude, Michele, Nathanael, Raegan, Renee, Sandra, Suzanna, Tina, Ulessia, Yvette, and more. These are Giant supermarket cashiers that help in my adventures. Their excitement and enthusiasm help me to keep going when I want to quit. It is not my nature to walk up to people and start talking, but God stretches me and takes me to levels that I never expected.

Pastors, Preachers, and teachers who have influenced my life, not in any specific order:

Curt & Pam Seaburg, Steve & Kim Crutchfield, Chris Smeltz, Brett Rush, Paul & Patty Peterson, Austin Karick, Joel Buffington, Rick Glass, Jeff Bender, Josh & Jaclyn Harnish, Cody Stoneback. Sam & Sherlyn Smucker, Don & Doris Neff, Cliff Martin, Amos Diener, Matt Mylan, Gordon & Nancy Groff, Dave Parker, Richard Armstrong, Worship Center Bible school teachers, Barry and Donna Ryan, Melody Day Martin, Ruby Jones. Eugene & Doris Wenger, Leon & Rosalee Schnupp, Norman Shenk, Andrew Miller, Leroy Hoover, Glenn Wonders. John Lindell, David Lindell, Brandon Lindell, Bill Johnson, Vlad Savchuk, Dr. David Jeremiah, John Bevere, Jonathan Cahn, Robert Henderson, Lance Wallnau, Gordon Mularski, Steven Furtick, Kris Valloton, John Hagee, Shane Wilson, James Epperly, Rick Warren.

There are many more names I could mention! I've been a Christian for 52 years. That's a lot of sermons!

1 Corinthians 15:58 NIV

Therefore, my dear brothers and sisters, stand firm. Let nothing move you. Always give yourselves fully to the work of the Lord, because you know that your labor in the Lord is not in vain.

CHAPTER 1
Finding purpose in your pain

While doing some research on Parkinson's, I came across this saying, "Pain Can Awaken A Profound Sense Of Meaning And Purpose." (psychologytoday.com) Finding purpose in your pain is an essential part of healing. You may never understand why such pain, or why this disease, or why your particular situation. Indeed, the randomness of life can be maddening, but what is important is deciding how you choose to live with your painful experience.

My wife, Karen, shared this with me: Experience is not what happens to you. It's what you do with what happens to you.

With Parkinson's, I've seen a lot of people who just give up. Now they are victims of the disease. That's why I wrote this book. To encourage people to choose a better outlook. Find your purpose! Don't go down without a fight! You will hear me say repeatedly, you were created on purpose, with a purpose, for a purpose. When you find out who you really are in Christ, and why God created you, you wouldn't want to be anybody, but you!

I am not downplaying anybody's challenges or medical conditions. Personally, I know the pain! I know the struggles and at times it can be horrific. Some days I can walk, some days I can run, and some days I can soar. I am grateful for each day.

Isaiah 40:31 NIV
But those who hope in the LORD will renew their strength. They will soar on wings like eagles; they will run and not grow weary, they will walk and not be faint.

Zach Williams has a song called "Less like me." The song goes, "Somebody with a hurt that I could've helped, somebody with a hand that I could've held. Let me be just a little more like Jesus, and a little less like me."

Sometimes that's all it takes. Holding somebody's hand while they hurt. Cry with them! Pray with them!

Whatever your medical condition, whatever your challenge, live it with purpose. Even with Parkinson's, love is free! It is the richest thing you can give away, and it doesn't cost you a penny. You can minister with or without finances. Just be the hands and feet of Jesus right where you are.

CHAPTER 2
Real people, real stories

As I tell my stories, there will be an infusion of my good days and my bad days. Yes, there are times that I just don't feel like it. For me, and many others, the reality of Parkinson's can be devastating, but God's grace is sufficient. If He calls you to do something, He will equip you for it. At the time it might seem impossible, but He will make a way. As I tell my stories, I might give you a glimpse of what I'm going through on that particular day, so that you know that I must rely on God to carry out His plan. Each day is a test of our faithfulness to Him, revealing His faithfulness to us. We are not required to get it right or perfect. God is only asking us to yield. He will do the rest.

I am part of a small group that discusses the Sunday sermon. What one person heard in the sermon may not be what the other person heard. Some of what they hear might be the same, but most of it is different. The Holy Spirit allows us to hear what we need for that moment in time. I guess what I'm trying to say is, allow yourself to be used every day, without trying to be perfect. You will make mistakes! I have included some of my mistakes in my stories. I am not a perfect man, and I do not try to be. If I try and fail, then I try again. I made a lot of mistakes in my carpentry career. I had to choose to learn from them, even if they were costly. You can't get better if you don't try. If you don't fail, what do you measure yourself against? As our children grow, we watch them try and fail, try, and succeed. It's all part of growing. We hurt from within when they fail, we rejoice when they succeed. That is a parent's heart. That is also God's heart. He will not protect us from pain or keep us from failing, that is part of growing. He sets a path before us. His intention is for our best, and to further His kingdom. If we pray, Your kingdom come, Your will be done, and we don't do anything, are we being blasphemous? We can't expect God to do it all when He placed us here to do it. Remember, it's His plan, and His purpose for you. You were designed on purpose, with a purpose, for a specific purpose.

My goal in this book is to show you how I would put action to what I was feeling or sensing. Example, if I felt a nudge to pull into a parking lot, I would do so. You will see several stories where I've done this and ended up helping somebody. Sometimes it's a test, sometimes somebody is waiting for their prayer to be answered. It is a process. Let me rephrase, it is a lifelong process. Don't ever expect God to always do it the same way. He just might change it up to see if you are listening. The only thing that remains the same is God's faithfulness. The challenge is for you to be open to hearing His voice.

You might get it right; you might get it wrong. Success comes on the heels of failure. In the kingdom of God, obedience is priceless. Can He trust you? Can you trust Him? By the end of this book, you should be encouraged to reach beyond your challenges and have mercy on others. Hopefully, you'll be strengthened in your purpose in life. My prayer is that you will fulfill your days with the purpose that God intended.

Your greatest witness to people is your story! What God has done for you can't be minimalized. Your story is what bears witness to others. Nobody can argue with your story. God has given you a message and no one can take it from you. You are on a journey. You are continuing your story. How it ends is up to you. Move forward with God's grace. Your best witness to an unbeliever is to tell your story. You can blow their minds.

My prayer is that you learn to enjoy the journey.

CHAPTER 3
Blazing a trail without a father's guidance

My life story is a testament to a loving and merciful God. I finally reached a point in life where I stopped fighting against what God wrote in my book about me.

October 29, 1973, my father Everett Leroy Williams passed away of a heart attack at age 49.

I had just started my senior year of high school when my father died. I did not cry or shed one tear. The next day I went to school as if nothing happened. I gazed out the window of the school bus as if to thank God that it was all over. Students and teachers were all asking, why aren't you at home mourning your loss? I did not answer. What was there to mourn? It had been sixteen years of a father's anger and physical/emotional abuse. My mother would get beatings on a weekly basis. We five kids would hide in the closet or under the bed. Was my father's behavior from the stress from fighting two wars? He was in the Army, the Navy, and the Air Force. I can't imagine the things that he saw while in combat. Although he was a war hero decorated with many medals, he was not a father figure or hero to his family. His death brought freedom! The anguish was over, but the hardship continued. I had to go to work to help support the family. At that time, we lived on a farm. I worked early in the morning and late in the evening. I would go to high school in the morning after the farm chores, then I would work in the afternoon and evening. I was fortunate to be in vocational technical school at the time. They allowed me to work half a day in place of vo-tech. My mother worked full-time and had five kids to support. My younger sister was pregnant and not married. With all this, I still managed to graduate while staying on the honor roll.

This was my typical day:
5:00 AM get up and feed the animals.
7:00 AM quick breakfast and off to school.
8:00 AM classes at high school
11:30 AM quick lunch at school
12:00 PM go to the job site and work until 5 o'clock.
6:00 PM evening chores on the farm.
8:00 PM study/homework for school.
10:00 PM wash up/go to bed.
5:00 AM repeat

I was weary and broken, blazing a trail without a father's guidance. Without my father's full-time income, we could no longer afford the farmhouse rent. We did the farm chores to offset the price of the house rental. On

January first, the rent went up, so my mother found a mobile home to live in. She could only take the two youngest children with her. My older brother dropped out of school and stayed with a friend. My pregnant sister married her boyfriend. I found an apartment on a neighboring farm. After working from noon to 5:00, I would work at that farm for extra money.

My mother, now without her husband, was single, supporting two children, but separated from three of them. Hardship for all, but with peace of mind:

No more emotional abuse.
No more beatings.
No more mental abuse, wondering if dad's cheating again.
No more fear of getting locked in the basement as punishment.
No more raging anger.

I made a vow never to be like my dad! Never hit a woman. Never have raging anger.

Looking back, around age 12, I gave my life to Christ. As a child we attended Saint Mark's United Methodist Church in Mount Joy. During a revival meeting I went up front and gave my life to Christ. My father did too. He was a changed man for a few months, and then slipped back into his old ways. I remember the day he made fun of a coworker who said he saw the light, and from that point on it was all downhill spiritually. As a teenager I made friends with a fellow carpenter who invited me to his church youth group. I recommitted myself to Christ at that time. The leaders of the youth group told me that God promises to be a father to the fatherless and I sure needed to hear that. There was a long road ahead for me, trying to get things right while not having a role model or father.

In 1976, at age 20, only a Christian for four years, I married. It was a constant battle for the next 12 years. Not having a role model, not knowing how to be a spiritual man, I made a lot of mistakes. Forgivable mistakes, I might add. I was trying to be scriptural, trying to enjoy life. After twelve years of me not being able to please her or her family, she asked for a divorce. I didn't understand! I was happy with our family and my accomplishments as a husband and a father. At that time, it was probably the saddest day in my life. I stayed single for 12 years. I was trying to work on me as a man while making massive alimony payments and living out of my truck. I was trying to keep my dignity intact. I could not afford an apartment after paying for child support, food, insurance, truck payments, and repairs. I was in a spiritual desert, braving the wilderness and going around the mountain again and again, feeling like I'm going it alone. I did not know it at the time, but God was building character and guiding me on my path. At that time, sitting under the teaching of the leadership team at The Worship Center, God was saturating me with His knowledge, creating in me a clean heart, renewing my spirit, and preparing me for the next phase of my journey. I have been on ten mission trips out of the country. I attended Worship Center Bible School for two years in 2000/2001. This is where I met the love of my life. Now I have been married to Karen for 24 years, wondering what's next? One day at a time, the journey continues. It's funny that I am writing this book while fulfilling the book that God wrote for me.

Psalm 139:16 ESV
Your eyes saw my unformed substance; in your book were written, every one of them, the days that were formed for me, when as yet there was none of them.

CHAPTER 4
Learning life's lessons

I was in the tenth grade. I was attending vocational technical training to be a carpenter. I decided I was going to build a better doghouse for our Labrador retriever. Our dogs were kept outside and needed shelter during bad weather. I set up an area in our basement as a shop. I built a really nice doghouse, but there was something inherently wrong: I could not get it through the basement door! I did not think to measure the door before I built the doghouse. I guess I can consider that a life lesson. I ended up removing the roof of the doghouse, to get it out of the basement. I felt foolish. I just didn't think it through.

Luke 14:28-29 MSG
Is there anyone here who, planning to build a new house, doesn't first sit down and figure the cost so you'll know if you can complete it? If you only get the foundation laid and then run out of money, you're going to look foolish.

This was the beginning of many projects of renovations and new construction. I had a 45-year career in carpentry. My final act was purchasing a house that needed total renovation when I was 60 years of age. The house was built in the 70s. After two weeks of removing the paneling, suspended ceiling, and shag carpeting, the house, now gutted to the studs, was ready to renovate.

What a way to enter retirement. It seemed like the projects never ceased. It kept me busy and kept me strong. This was to be our forever home in our retirement.

Things ended abruptly about six years later when I was diagnosed with Parkinson's. I had an uncontrollable tremor that interfered with projects and maintenance. It seemed kind of ironic that after losing 50 pounds and teaching health strategies to others, that I came down with Parkinson's. We were sure it was from my many years of job-site chemical exposure to things like pesticides, herbicides, industrial solvents, and others. I was told that the products were safe, and I didn't protect myself. Yet what seemed to be another devastating blow, turned out to be a springboard to a ministry of compassion and generosity. This ministry was something I could never do on my own but had to rely on God for every move I made.

Romans 8:18 RSV

I consider that the sufferings of this present time are not worth comparing with the glory that is to be revealed to us.

CHAPTER 5
Where did it begin?

People ask where my ministry began. Well, it's hard to say. I guess it had become a lifestyle and I just didn't know it. I'll take you back to a story in 2020 before I had Parkinson's. I was starting to learn how to rest in God's timing while paying attention to the nudges or promptings in my spirit. I noticed a pattern with things happening after I felt the nudge. When I would pay attention to the nudge and act accordingly, people would be waiting for an answer to their prayer. There were times where I did not pay attention to the nudge and would shrug it off, but then my heart would feel heavy. At that point, I knew I missed God's purpose for the nudge. Sometimes wondering what I missed, I would turn around, go back to where I felt the nudge, and find somebody needing help.

Here's a story about the nudge. My wife asked me to do a small project at her work. I needed to remove tools out of the back of my truck to complete this task. While I was preparing my truck, I came across an old marine fire extinguisher. My first impression was to take it out of the truck bed, but in my gut, I felt I should set it aside in the corner where I could reach it.

I finished the work that I was commissioned for that day. As I closed my truck cap, I caught a glimpse of the fire extinguisher in the corner where I left it. As I was driving, I noticed people slowing down and getting into the left lane. They were passing a pick-up truck with flammable materials on fire in the truck bed. I waited for him to pull over, and then I pulled in front of him. I grabbed the fire extinguisher and handed it to him. There was just enough in the extinguisher to put the fire out. After a sigh of relief, we talked for a while. I told him my story of the fire extinguisher. We agreed it was a God thing.

That night, as I wrote in my journal, I felt the presence of God. This was not a coincidence! This is where hearing God is important if you are going to successfully help people.

CHAPTER 6
Another story, from 2021

I had no idea where I was going. It was a very cold morning. I drove until my heart felt satisfied, then I stopped and parked. I got out of my truck and looked around. I started walking down the path along the river, enjoying the view, but not knowing why I was there. I came across a guy in a chair, all bundled up, looking at the river. I walked up to him and stood beside him for a minute. Then I asked him if this was a good place to meet God? That started the conversation.

I noticed by now that he had tears in his eyes, and not from the cold. We talked for a while and then I asked him what I could do for him. He wanted me to pray that he would have peace. So, I did. He was an interim pastor who was affected by the world of Covid. He was in the middle of making some decisions and needed some clarity. He drove a long way to this particular spot. God knew right where he was. God knew exactly what he needed. He sent me, without a clue where I was going, to walk down a path, and ask him a simple question.

I guess you never know where you will find God. Be assured of this one thing, He always knows where you are!

Psalm 16:8 NLT
I know the Lord is always with me. I will not be shaken, for He is right beside me.

CHAPTER 7
Forever changed, my turnaround story

I spent my first six months of Parkinson's chasing answers. My life was consumed from my world being turned upside down. I wanted this disease to be removed. I did not like this mountain or the challenge. It was too painful.

Truly, my God could heal me in a second, but would that be beneficial to His plan? What did He want me to learn through this? I was not willing to find out. When the mountain was not removed, what choice did I have? I felt that the word of God had no power.

As the illness progressed, I started to crumble, both physically and spiritually. I begged God to heal me. His ears were closed to my request. Then the day came when God showed me His plan. I was listening to a message* that struck my soul in a way that forever changed me. The raw emotion of someone else's pain sent chills through my body. The testimony of her journey brought peace to my heart. What is God really doing? I was about to find out.

I released my will and accepted His plan. Then the journey began. I asked God to give me purpose in my pain. He gave me empathy for others. He showed me that He could use me despite my disease. I had to lean on Him daily, learn His voice, and go where He sent me. The journey of obedience had opened my world to a new purpose. In this book, you will see what God accomplished in two and a half years.

* Notes and highlights from that message:

Bread for today, seed for tomorrow. Getting past the disappointment.
No longer begging God to take it away.
Hope from the seeds of yesterday's experience with God.
The word is my source of hope.
Getting alone with God, anchoring my heart to what I did know was certain.
Knowing that there is a purpose in my pain.

Message reference:
21 Days of Prayer and Fasting
Hold on But Don't Hold Still
January 2, 2022 • Pam Seaburg
https://victorychurch.org/resources/messages

Hebrews 10:35-36 NLT
So do not throw away this confident trust in the Lord. Remember the great reward it brings you!

Patient endurance is what you need now, so that you will continue to do God's will. Then you will receive all that He has promised.

During your crisis, the word of God, loaded with His promises, becomes your anchor. The spoken word feeds you and gives you hope. His words are your bread for today and your seed for tomorrow. The Word of God is the material that the Holy Spirit uses to build your spiritual life.

CHAPTER 8
My new outlook on life

I had a new outlook on life after hearing that message. Anxious to start the journey, I would get up in the morning and pray for discernment.

In the back of my mind, I was pondering, would this be the day that I get my healing? Anticipating that God is about to do great things to me and through me. Now I was seeking to get closer to the one who can heal, not seeking the healing. If it didn't happen, I knew He would empower me, despite my medical condition.

Then as my day continued, I waited for the nudge to drive. I get in my truck, not knowing what direction to go or who to help. At this point, I didn't need any money for what He called me to do. All I had to do was listen and act upon it. Once I got better at listening, God started showing me people who needed financial assistance. When I started, I could afford one gift card a month. As I was faithful, God gave me more.

Most days I get up in the morning not knowing what the adventure will be. There are days that I get it wrong. But more times than not, I get it right.

So, what will it be for you? Will you walk into a nursing home and befriend somebody? Will you ask your neighbors what you can do to make their life better? Will you take a meal to your neighbor, or the homeless person who stands on the corner? Can you offer a sleeping bag or a hat, gloves, or sweatshirt? Will you ask someone if they need help paying for their gas, groceries, rent, car payment, childcare, or medical bill? How can you make someone's life a little easier? When you see people crying, talk with them, pray with them, or just hold their hands and comfort them. Who knows? It just might take you on the adventure of a lifetime.

The thrill that you get from helping somebody is beyond measure. The rewards in heaven are waiting. God is ready to open the floodgates as you act on scripture. It is endless, how many ways you can be a blessing. Don't look at your condition and say that you can't. Send a text of encouragement. Call someone and say that you were thinking about them.

Opportunities are around you every day. Are you looking? Are you hearing? Are you listening? It's not that God isn't speaking, but are you hearing? You may have heard God speak, but did you listen to what was being said? Listening is an exercise of faith. Trust me when I say you can get it wrong as many times as you can get it right. You can start as soon as you say that you are available.

You say, "but it's not easy." or "I can't do that." God didn't make it easy, He made it so that you would trust Him to give you the strength. Step out in faith. Start with sharing your testimony. We all have one! We have all come through something that was hard. Maybe it's time to write a book!

CHAPTER 9
God things

Today I went to my wife's place of business to help her with a project. After a few hours, I looked up and knew it was time to leave. The Holy Spirit was prompting me to move on to my next divine appointment. I went to say goodbye to my wife to tell her I had "God things" to attend to. As I was saying goodbye, there was a lady at the counter buying a lock and she couldn't find her money. I stepped in and paid for it. Her comment was, "Just as I was losing faith in all humanity, you stepped in and did this for me. Thank you." She proceeded to say that somebody did her wrong and somebody else called her ugly as she was walking down the sidewalk. We assured her that God loves her.

Then I headed towards my favorite place, Columbia, Pennsylvania! Over the years I found different ways to make a difference in this town. Today was no exception. As I got off the ramp at Columbia, I recognized the homeless man that I minister to on a weekly basis. I pulled over and handed him some money. His face lights up when I call him by name. I reassured him that God has his back if he will trust in Him.

Victory Church has a campus in Columbia. Karen and I started attending there when we lived in Wrightsville. I started getting involved with the homeless shelter and serving meals. Then I started taking it to the streets and ministering to the homeless people who did not come to the shelter. I started by getting to know their names and bringing them whatever they needed to survive. Once you get to know them, and call them by name, it's a whole new paradigm. When they know that you care, they want to hear what you have to say.

I got to know this homeless guy outside of the restaurant at the Giant shopping center, just around the corner from where he stands at the exit ramp asking for help. His story is legitimate. He was injured and has a disability. He has been waiting for the long process of disability payments to go through. In the meantime, nobody will hire him because of this. I started buying him breakfast and listening to his stories. He is always humbled when he sees me, especially when I call him by name. The homeless people need to be heard. They need to be loved.

Next, I stopped at Giant to pick up four gift cards at $50 each. I walked through the store and quickly realized that this wasn't where I was supposed to be. Normally I hand the gift cards out in the store. Today was different.

I got back in my truck with the gift cards and headed towards my church. Not knowing what was next, I saw a couple at my church campus handing out free food for kids' lunches. I walked up to them, asked for, and heard their story. They had a friend whose house burned down. I gave them all four cards. One for them for being faithful to their calling and three for the family they spoke about. Tears were shed.

I remember a few months ago just starting with one gift card, all I could afford. Even that was a stretch for some months. But I knew people needed help. I saw a lady looking at groceries and putting them back. After a few minutes, I realized she couldn't afford everything that she needed. I purchased a gift card and handed it to her a little later. The tears and comments reassured me that it was needed. As time went on, I would buy an occasional card and ask God who: who needs it, who should I give it to? Now I typically go to the gift card rack and ask God how many before I walk through the store.

As a person with Parkinson's, I find that giving gift cards is a very convenient way to help people and it is very rewarding. I used to help people with projects around the house, but I can no longer offer services like that due to my handicap. As my physical limitations changed, I had to adapt to how to minister to people. I had to adapt to how to have purpose in this world.

Next, I ordered a pizza and went to pick it up. I didn't know what I was going to do with the pizza. That's what I heard God tell me to do. As I entered the store there was a gentleman waiting for his pizza, but mine was ready. So, I paid for mine, gave a tip, and turned to the guy. I offered to pay for his pizza. He gladly accepted. We talked for a while, then he went his way.

Still having my pizza in hand, I headed down to River Park. I walked up to a gentleman carrying a backpack. I asked him if he wanted a pizza for lunch. He accepted and began eating. As I walked away, I heard someone say to him, "Well, my friend, you said you didn't know what you were going to have for lunch today. Now you're having lunch." Apparently, he just got done telling somebody he didn't know what he was going to do for lunch. I assume that he was homeless.

I looked up to heaven and smiled at God. It's amazing that if you just take the steps, God provides the adventures.

CHAPTER 10
After breakfast, I enjoyed some alone time with God

I decided that I'm going to rest in my situation with Parkinson's, and trust in how God chooses to use me. Around noon time I felt the prompting, "to go." I usually second-guess myself as to if there's a mission involved. I decided to park my truck under a shade tree at the grocery store and walk some extra steps, not knowing at that time where I parked was critical to blessing somebody. Walking helps to improve my Parkinson's tremor. I went inside to get some groceries and gift cards.

While I was waiting in line to pay, my eyes connected with a toddler who was beeping the horn on his shopping cart. His mom was shopping in the aisle behind me. He was looking right at me while beeping. I made a noise back to him like I was beeping. We giggled and had fun. Then they went their way. I bought four gift cards at $50 each. Why $50? I don't know .... could you use $50? It seems like an OK amount. I know there's somebody in the store who could use an extra $50.

Earlier, when I was getting my bananas, I saw a young mother training her two children to shop with their tiny carts. She had a great attitude towards letting them grab the bananas and put them in the cart. It's great to see when a loving mother spends time with her children. I wanted to bless her with a card but lost track of her in the store.

After I checked out, I put my groceries in my truck. Suddenly, I noticed that I did not have my gift cards. It took me a few minutes to find them buried in one of the grocery bags. I took my cart back to the corral where I met up with the lady with the kids. I'm thinking, "what great timing, God! You are awesome." I proceeded to tell her that I had noticed how she interacted with her children. I asked her if I could bless her with a $50 gift card and she immediately started to cry. I knew God was loving on her. She thanked me, and I departed with a smile. Oh God I love what you're up to! Had I not parked where I did, and lost track of my gift cards for a few minutes, the timing would not have been so perfect.

Next time you lose track of something, ask God what He's up to! When you don't get that perfect parking spot just chuckle, knowing that God has your back.

I headed back into the store to give away the other cards, knowing that God was blessing people. I saw a man shopping with his three children. I felt like I should stop, but I made a pre-judgment about him, thinking that he wouldn't accept. I went on my way but didn't get far when God turned me around. As I approached the man, he was now with his wife and the rest of his children.

Wow, I thought this family could probably use it. "Sir, may I ask you a question?" He said, "sure." I asked, "would it be beneficial to you if your family had another $50 towards your groceries?" He said, "absolutely. What must I do?" I said, "just receive it." He shook my hand, thanked me, and said, "God bless you, brother."

As I was getting ready to leave, I saw a grandmother with her daughter and two grandchildren. Each grandchild had their own cart in training. I looked at grandma and said, "I would like to talk to you. I love to see how you take an interest in your grandchildren." She said, "I love them dearly." I asked if I may bless her with a $50 gift card. "Sure! That would be great." She gave me a hug, we talked a bit, and I went on my way.

I went outside towards my truck and noticed the lady that I had seen previously with her toddler in her cart (beep beep). She was getting into her car, and I asked her if I could bless her with a card. At first, she was skeptical but received it graciously. When she saw the amount on it, I could see her eyes light up. She thanked me, and I went on my way.

Right now, I feel like doing the happy dance! Thank you, God, for using me. There are so many people hurting financially. A little bit of blessing goes a long way!

CHAPTER 11
Make a difference!

Victory Church made a T-shirt that says, "Make A Difference." This morning, I put on my T-shirt to do just that!

I got in my truck and headed to Giant in Mount Joy, with no agenda other than getting a pineapple and some bananas. As I walked into the store, I felt drawn towards the cash registers. I'm thinking, "already? Who is it today?"

I saw a young lady with a child in the cart putting a lot of groceries on the conveyor belt, dozens of cans of soup. Must be a big family, I thought. I walked around the cash register and asked the young lady if I could pay for all her groceries. She said, "that would be great, but only if you want to." That sounded like scripture to me. You can heal me, Jesus, if you want to! "Yes, I want to." She proceeded to tell me her story of about an hour ago, she had to leave her groceries behind. Her credit cards were missing from the back of her cell phone. She was embarrassed. She put her groceries back in the cart and went home to find her credit cards. Now that she had returned, I was offering to pay for them. God is so good, turning the bad into good.

This lady and her husband had adopted six children. The one with her had an older sibling. They adopted them together so they wouldn't be separated. Groceries are a big expense for this family. I like blessing people like that. I really felt God rewarded her for what she's doing.

Thanks again, Father, for using me. Thank you, Father, for putting me here to make a difference.

My wife, Karen, and I normally sit down for a game together before we go to bed. With my Parkinson's I'm supposed to try to walk more. I asked her to go for a walk instead of a game. When we take walks, we have a normal walking routine in our community. I broke from that routine, not knowing God was up to something. Halfway through the walk I normally make a left turn and head home. I decided to make a right turn and push myself a little harder with some extra steps. As we made the final turn towards home, we came across a neighbor who was excited to see us. She had talked with Karen a few weeks back. Karen did not realize she had laid a foundation for a new friendship. We shared some things with her, and she asked for prayer for her husband. Wow! If we had gone a different way to please my flesh, we would have missed out on this opportunity.

CHAPTER 12
Necessary detour

Yesterday I got something in the mail which required my attention today. It was around 11 o'clock that I thought, I really need to take care of this. So I stopped what I was doing, dropped off the paperwork and headed home. It was now 11:45 and I was almost home when I got the nudge to head to Columbia. I thought to myself, I should have taken the previous exit to save time. I felt like I wasted about 8 to 10 minutes of my time taking the long way around, not realizing that the detour was necessary for me to meet the right people at the right time. If I'd thought about it sooner, and taken a different way, I may have missed my opportunity. God's timing is so much better than our minds could ever comprehend. His orchestration of several divine appointments at the same destination, to me, is just awesome. God was setting me up to bless four families today.

As I walked in the doors of Giant in Columbia, the Holy Spirit directed me to a young man pushing his kids around in a grocery cart. I could see he was being selective in the food he was choosing. Could money have been an issue?

I proceeded to buy four gift cards valued at $50 each. The elderly cashier who waited on me now knows my name. Her name is Kathleen. She's all smiles when I come walking her way. We talked about the mission that I'm on, and she is just so thrilled that I do this. One day she flat out asked me what I did with all the cards I bought because she saw me walking through the store handing them out. She even got bold enough one day to tell me that the person behind me had a bad situation and could use one. I took her advice, turned around and gave it to the lady behind me. She started to weep and tell me her story. I started out by buying gift cards at the Giant store in Columbia. When we moved to Mt. Joy, I continued there.

I took a small cart and my bag of gift cards and started to walk through the store. I try to listen to the leading of the Holy Spirit.

The man I had talked about earlier was the first one that I came across. I asked him if it would be a help to have an extra $50 towards groceries this week. He said that would be great! I gave him the card and he had his children thank me. We talked for a bit, shook hands, and went our way. While I was walking away, under my breath I said "God, thank you for letting me do this, I love helping others."

Just down the next aisle was a young lady with her toddler and a shopping cart full of food. I said, "pardon me young lady." She said, "yes." I asked, "would it be beneficial to you if you had an extra $50 to go towards your grocery bill?" She said, "that would be awesome, how do I get it?" I replied, "just receive it."

And she did. She wanted an explanation. I explained to her that this is what my wife and I do for people. We hand out gift cards to bless people as they raise their families. She was very appreciative. We talked a bit and then I moved on.

During my single years I knew what it was like to struggle financially trying to put food on the table. I remember the times I just bought necessities. There wasn't extra money to eat out. It became even more real after I injured my back and couldn't work. I couldn't do any side hustles because of the injury. Where would the extra money come from? I made too much money to collect from food banks or government assistance. But there wasn't any money. Finding ways to hold it together became my reality. My weaknesses became my tests in life. After I overcame my struggles, my test eventually became my testimony. Whose pain do you feel? That's who you are drawn to, so you can help. When I walk into a grocery store and see someone clipping a coupon, or putting food back, I take that as a sign for me to help. If I can help ease the burden of someone's struggle, even for a day, it is worth it.

God then proceeded to nudge me to the produce section. I had already been in the produce section, but I obeyed. There was another young man with his two children just starting to do their shopping. I asked him the same question. Would it be of benefit to you and your family to receive a $50 gift card towards your purchase? He looked around and then said to me, "how do I do that?" I explained that we like to help growing families with grocery bills. We proceeded to chitchat about life. He thanked me and asked me if he could give me a hug. I shook his hand and gave him a hug.

I had one more card to give away and I saw a family that I had blessed months ago. They were there at the start of my grocery ministry about a year ago. I hadn't seen them in a while. I met up with them a few aisles down. Much to my surprise she was very pregnant. I opened with "Long time no see! How have you been?" We both chuckled as she looked at her belly, now looking like she's in her final month. She told me she was having a girl, and the family is growing! I replied well I know she is in good hands because I watch how loved and well-behaved your other children are. She was almost in tears because she knew what was happening. I gave her the final gift card that I had. When we ended the conversation, I headed towards my truck. This is one thing that I can do that isn't hindered by Parkinson's. Now fully exhausted, I headed home for a nap.

Thank you, God, for trusting me to bless people. Thank you for the financial resources to do so. Thank you for a church that preaches how to hear from You and to do something! Thank you for taking the time to speak to me personally and using me for Your greater plan.

CHAPTER 13
Down but not done! There is still work to do

After my doctor's appointment today, I went for blood tests. It's hard to drive when I feel nauseated and dizzy. God said to me today, "Do you trust me?" "Yes God, I do."

At that moment, my head was clear with no dizziness or nausea. He said, go to Columbia, pick up a pizza and go to the park. I was thinking, I haven't seen this guy in four weeks, but I did as I felt directed.

When I got there the homeless guy was sitting on the bench as I parked the truck. I called him by name, and he lit up like a Christmas tree. He shouted, "you remembered my name."

"Of course! I brought pizza for you, and I want to sit down with you and talk." We had a really good conversation for 45 minutes. After we got to know each other's background, he asked me how do I know what my purpose is? Why are we here? I told him that he was my purpose but on the flipside of the coin I am his purpose. He wanted me to explain. I said, "you are here to help build my character as a human being. You give me purpose in life to help, not only you, but others like you. And I am here to help you understand your purpose. Where you are now is not where you will stay. You may be here from your own decisions and mistakes. But I am here to help you realize you are more than that. The fact that you let me help you in your humility is building your character and fulfilling your purpose at this time in your life." I was thinking, where did that come from? But it hit him hard in his spirit. He then knew there was more to his life than where he is now. It was hard to make it through the next 10 minutes without crying. The seeds were planted. We developed a friendship. We agreed I would see him again tomorrow at noon to help him with a few necessities. All he wants right now is a tarp, so he doesn't get wet at night. Before I left, his last comment to me was this, "why is it that you do not look down on me?" I told him that I was homeless once in my life.

I shared with him the time that I was homeless after my first marriage ended. My alimony payments were so high I could not afford a place to live. As a father, I struggled with who I was as a person, still wanting to be a great dad. I lived out of my truck in a storage unit. I continued to work and support my kids while navigating the realm of homelessness. I did not want to become a statistic or a deadbeat dad. I loved my boys too much to abandon them. A convenience store employee, from my church at that time, offered free food. Someone else from church offered me the use of their motor home over the winter. That ended when spring came, and they wanted to use it. I appreciated their generosity and quickly found a place to stay in exchange for carpentry services.

As I look back, I can see God's hand on my life, the twists and turns that shaped who I am, coupled with the encouragement that I got from God's people. Now I choose to use that experience to encourage the homeless that God puts in my path.

By the time I got home, all my symptoms came back. I was so glad my head was clear to minister, trusting God one day at a time for my healing. After I got home, I thought about how I could not have choreographed such an event like this. God is awesome. To sit with a guy who has such humility in his situation was amazing.

All that I am and ever hope to be is because of Christ.

Philippians 4:11-13 NLT

Not that I was ever in need, for I have learned how to be content with whatever I have. I know how to live on almost nothing or with everything. I have learned the secret of living in every situation, whether it is with a full stomach or empty, with plenty or little. For I can do everything through Christ, who gives me strength.

CHAPTER 14
If they ask for your shirt, give them your coat also

I have seen a lot of doctors and had a lot of tests in the last two weeks. I've had vertigo and dizziness for over six weeks now. Some days I can't drive. I've been to the emergency room twice and did not get any relief. It feels as though my God has forsaken me. All this, on top of having Parkinson's, tremors, and a recent discovery of bradycardia, which is a low heart rate in the 40s. As of now I've had over 60 episodes in the 37 to 43 bpm range.

When I say it feels like my God has forsaken me, I know better, but it doesn't feel better. I had one good day last week where God was gracious, and I was able to minister to the homeless in Columbia. I keep getting drawn back to that area. I financially helped the man on the exit ramp. I like it when I get a red light so I can talk with him.

Today I went to the River Park area. When I got there to meet with my usual guy, he was accompanied by a homeless couple. He brought them along to hear about the good things that I was sharing with him, letting them know that there are two sides to every coin and that their lives matter to God. Letting them know that this is not just about them, it's also about the people who help them. They now understand that in their situation, they help God's people to become doers of the word.

After we talked for an hour, I asked them what I could do for them. If you spend time with them, they will let you know what they need. They said as it gets colder, they need things to keep them warm. We went to my truck, and I pulled out sweatshirts, gloves, knit caps, rain gear, and hand warmers. I was prepared to help one person with warm gear and ended up helping three. They were so grateful that someone cared. The Bible talks about giving the shirt off your back. I ended up giving not only the stuff I had prepared, but also my favorite sweatshirt, my Gore-Tex rain gear, and my lightweight rain jacket. There was more need than I anticipated, but I had enough to meet the need. God is good. God is gracious. Thank you, Father, for using me.

The next morning was bitterly cold, so I went back to see how they survived the night, but I only saw the girl. She cried when she saw me and I heard her say thank God, it's you! She asked if she could get in the truck to get warm. She was a mess.

I took her to the Presbyterian Church where they were doing free lunches for anybody. I saw some of my church friends handing out food. We're all in this together. I gave her more hand warmers and she went on her way. You never know if you're going to see them again.

God, please lead me through the winding roads that create the journey that is mine. Not somebody else's, but mine. I am created to touch souls. Lead me to souls that are hurting. Let me be a light to them, and continue my mission with my head held high, and my hands stretched out. Amen.

Psalm 84:6 TPT
Even when their paths wind through the dark valley of tears, they dig deep to find a pleasant pool where others find only pain. He gives to them a brook of blessing filled from the rain of an outpouring.

Pray for me, while I find out what's wrong with my body. I know my God can heal me with just one touch.

CHAPTER 15
God is up to more than I know

It was supposed to be a quick stop at the store and get home. I didn't feel like interacting with people today! My Parkinson's tremor had flared up again. But God is gracious in moments like this. I used to say, "this disease robbed my ability to do things for God." Now I realize it has opened a new world of boldness and prayer.

I got the items I needed and decided to pick up two gift cards in case I needed them (and I did!). I only bought two cards today, because finances are tight. However, Karen and I are faithful in tithing, and we trust God for the harvest. Tithing is first and foremost in our marriage, giving back to God the first fruits. Then He will guide us on how to spend the rest. Tithing is ten percent of our income which we give to our church. When we give away gift cards, that is above our tithe. There are weeks that I can't buy gift cards because of the cost of Parkinson's. There are many tests and procedures that are not covered by insurance. I can't do medications due to my allergies to dyes and fillers. That makes out-of-pocket expenses higher than normal. I have realized that if I don't take care of myself, I won't be able to help anybody else. So, there are times when I can't buy gift cards *and* pay for tests in the same week.

With my two gift cards, I felt that I needed to go back through the store, even though I had paid for my groceries. I came across a young mother with an infant in her cart. I asked her if it would be OK if I gave her a gift card to help with the groceries. She replied, "don't mess with me, I could get very emotional over that."
I said, "go ahead!" Then I proceeded to give her the gift card. She got all teary-eyed. I told her it was OK. Once she was comforted, I went on my way.

The second encounter set me back a little bit. I expect everyone to say yes, but every now and then someone says no. She told me she felt that her family had been blessed, and I could give it to someone else who could use it more. She said she appreciated the thought and admired me for what I was doing. She commented that she would like to do that too, but had not started. I thanked her for her honesty and proceeded to find someone else.

I came across another lady with a young child by her side. I previously judged her and passed her by because I thought she would not receive it, yet our paths crossed again, almost as if God had orchestrated it! I asked her if I could bless her with a $50 gift card towards the purchase of her groceries. She received it, thanked me, and got very emotional. She looked me straight in the eyes and said, "you have no idea what this means."

I replied, "I may not, but God does! He's looking out for you." She thanked me again and continued to cry. I told her it was OK as I comforted her. Then I said goodbye to her and her child.

As I turned the corner, I saw the lady who turned me down. I told her she had great insight and thanked her for turning me down because now there was another person who was grateful for the help. We talked some more on how she'd like to do this kind of thing for other people. She looked at me and said that I was such an inspiration to her. She said, "I want to go home and ask my husband if we can do this too." At that moment, I realized that it's not just about me, it's about encouraging others to be like Jesus. I'm learning to be open to every person in front of me and not being so quick to judge by what I see. Some people hide their hurts and needs very well.

Heavenly Father, Thank You for the teaching of Your word. Thank You for those who teach us and those who lead by example. Amen

Hebrews 13:16 ESV
Do not neglect to do good and to share what you have, for such sacrifices are pleasing to God.

CHAPTER 16
Verifying my ministry

I march to the beat of a different drum, so I'm told.

My sister-in-law, San, enjoys my chili and zucchini bread. Recently, I started making tuna salad. She says that's her favorite. I took some to her this morning. Since her husband passed away, my brother-in-law, Terry, and I, and our wives, have helped her clean the inside of her house, power wash the sidewalks, install flashing, caulk areas where rain got inside the basement, clean out the garage, and more. She took care of her husband for the last three years of his life. He wasn't the same after he had a bad fall and hit his head. She was recently hospitalized with a heart condition, stressed out from taking care of him. Now we are helping her.

When I left San's house, I headed to Giant to get a few things. While I was at the grocery store, I felt impressed to approach a young lady with a minimal number of groceries in her cart. As I watched, she looked at groceries but did not put them in her cart. I assumed she was deciding what was affordable. I asked her if I could help her with her purchase today. She replied, "whatever is in your heart." I really liked that answer! I gave her a $50 gift card. A little bit of small talk, then I walked away.

I proceeded to the checkout. After purchasing my groceries, the cashier, a few rows over, flagged me down. I went over to talk to her. She was so excited. "I just had one of your gift cards come through this line! The customer said, 'a man just walked up to me and blessed me with this gift card. I don't think he knows how much I need that." And I told her, "I think he does."

I was so excited, I took my groceries to the truck, and realized I did not get McDonald's cards as my wife requested. I went back in and got 16 gift cards for the homeless and two more Giant gift cards. I tried to give one away to an elderly lady. She said, "no, I'm doing just fine." Then she looked at me intensely and said, "is this your ministry?" Oh, did that open the door for good conversation! She was excited to talk about God. It was refreshing to have a Godly person verify my ministry.

I left there with a spring in my step or something closely resembling it! (Parkinson's walk isn't pretty).

With the recent sermons that we've had at church about being generous, Karen told me about a way she wants to help the homeless. It's getting cold, so she's making care packages. Each bag will have a McDonald's gift card, a bottle of water, breakfast bars, hand warmers, and a pair of gloves. I'm excited for her new adventure. She listens to my stories all the time. Now I get to hear hers.

A special thanks to our church leadership for bringing challenging messages to us.

Proverbs 21:13 NLT

Those who shut their ears to the cries of the poor will be ignored in their own time of need.

CHAPTER 17
Let the glory fall!

Over the years, while buying gift cards to hand out at grocery stores, there have been a few key people in the know when I walk in. I would pick up a handful of gift cards to purchase. I'd walk to the information center and pay for them. At first, nobody knew my name or what I was up to. Now when they see me coming, they smile and get excited. They know that something exciting is about to happen, the glory of God is going to fall. People are going to be touched. Ministering angels will descend. Tears will be shed. Stories will be shared. Cashiers will smile. Lives will be changed.

When God is at work, I trust that He will give me the words to say in that moment. Sometimes it's a little, sometimes it's a lot. Most times it happens so fast that I must trust that the Holy Spirit will make up the difference from what is said or not said. I'm starting to see the bigger picture in all of this.

Today, just as I purchased the cards, I had an immediate opportunity. I asked a young lady with a child, already done with her purchase and heading for the exit, "could I bless you with a gift card for your next purchase?" She pondered the question and started to weep. Through her tears, she said, "yes," received the card and proceeded to tell me about their struggles. The cashier was in awe. "How do you know who to pick?" Sometimes I know, sometimes I don't! I trust people to tell me when they don't need it. It does happen. And then I thank them for their honesty. I do get it wrong at times, but I'd rather be wrong than not try at all.

The next person was a true set up by God. Her cart was blocking my ability to turn down the next aisle. I took the opportunity to speak. "May I ask you a question?" She scrambled trying to move her cart, realizing that she was in the way. I responded, "you are OK right where you are. As a matter of fact, you're in the right place at the right time." She hesitated, looking at me, wondering what I meant. "I would like to bless you with a gift card towards your purchase today."

She immediately started crying and slowly responded. "You don't know how much of a blessing that is! My husband's been sick, and we could use the money." I offered her a second card, but she declined. "This one is enough."

Minutes later, she shared her story with the cashier. Later, the cashier shared it with me. She said, "I knew immediately who she was talking about when she started talking about the gift card. I get to hear lots of stories because of you." God was using the cashier to tell others of His goodness. People were listening.

I approached an elderly lady in a motorized cart. She had a lot of items jammed in. I struck up a conversation with her. I started to ask if I could help financially, and immediately she said, "you may not pay for all my groceries! That's almost $200!" I offered this back to her, "how about I just help you with it? Here is a $50 gift card towards your purchase." "That I will accept! You're just not paying for the whole thing." I noticed that she was wearing a Jesus sweatshirt. I found out that she goes to a church in Elizabethtown, and she sings in the choir. She lives alone and struggles occasionally with finances. I think I made a new friend today!

Out of the corner of my eye, I saw a lady smiling at me with a thumbs up. She looked familiar, but I could not place her until suddenly it dawned on me: I gave her a gift card a few months back when she lost her job. I did not know she lost her job when I gave it to her. Only afterwards did she reveal that to me.

Just like a diamond has many facets, I'm starting to see there is more to this picture. In the beginning of my giving, it was just me wanting to help people. Giving is not just about a person giving or about the other person receiving a gift. It's about a person's attitude and spiritual posture when they give, creating an atmosphere for receiving, while enlisting others to participate and engaging bystanders who are watching. You could be an example or an inspiration to someone else wanting to do this. How many times have I heard, "I wish I could do that," or "I appreciate what you're doing for others."

Are you being a catalyst? Are you planting seeds? Are you being kind to others despite their unkindness? Can you get past not knowing what they are going through, so you can lift them up? Will you be the Jesus that they need today?

Ephesians 3:20 TPT

Never doubt God's mighty power to work in you and accomplish all this. He will achieve infinitely more than your greatest request, your most unbelievable dream, and exceed your wildest imagination! He will outdo them all, for His miraculous power constantly energizes you.

CHAPTER 18
Steppingstones

There is a long and winding road to finding your purpose. When you are trying to find your calling, and what your purpose is, first take heed to each steppingstone. Steppingstones create a path. Paths become trails. Trails become roads. Roads take you to your destiny.

Romans 5:3-4 NIV
Not only so, but we also glory in our sufferings, because we know that suffering produces perseverance; perseverance, character; and character, hope.

My Parkinson's journey is like a mountainous terrain. It started with little hills and valleys. The hills get bigger as I journey to my destination. The exercise from the little hills works my muscles and gives me strength for the bigger hills ahead of me. In the distance I can see the next hill and ponder how I'm ever going to get up to the top. But as I'm climbing that hill, I can't see the top.

I am "in the moment" where I'm at. Before I know it, I am at the top. I gained strength from the previous hills. But now I must go through the valley before I can climb the next hill. It's all necessary in gaining the strength that I need for the next challenge in my life. I am thankful for the mountains and valleys in my life, which in return give me the strength that I need to complete the journey. I need strength to finish well. May grace and mercy be my companion. Thanks, Lord, for the update in my spirit. Let me see when You carry me. And when You set me down, please point my feet in the right direction.

With my Parkinson's diagnosis there came a flood of other issues. Bradycardia, tachycardia, premature ventricular contractions, atrial fibrillation, vertigo, nystagmus, and a tremor in my dominant hand.

In James 5:14 the Bible says to call for the elders of the church and have them lay hands and pray for you, anoint you with oil, and you will be healed.

So that's what we did. Armed with Psalm 41 as my weapon, they prayed for me, and the tremor disappeared for two days! Then it came back as fierce as it was before. Chores and simple grooming tasks are almost impossible. I asked God why I couldn't keep my healing. This is what I heard God whisper to me. "For two days, I removed the tremor. I wanted you to know that I can do it, and I will do it, but the time is not yet. This will be for My glory! Many people have seen your plight and when you are healed, they will know that I am God your healer. Trust my timing and continue showing my love to others. My word will not return void!"

Psalm 41:1-3 AMP

Blessed is the one who considers the poor! In the day of trouble, the Lord delivers him; the Lord protects him and keeps him alive; he is called blessed in the land; You do not give him up to the will of his enemies. The Lord sustains him on his sick bed; in his illness You restore him to full health.

So, I encourage you to stop second-guessing and move on. There is no looking back, there are no do overs! Just keep your eye on the prize moving forward. Listen for the Holy Spirit to speak. He will take you on a journey as you could never have fathomed! The next time He says, "turn here," do it! Yes, DO IT!!

Here's an example. One day I felt strongly to 'turn here' so I pulled into the parking lot of a Kmart store. I proceeded to walk to the entrance of the building when my heart got heavy. "This isn't it" I said to myself. I turned around and started walking back to my truck. Frantically, I asked God, "Did I miss the mark?" My eyes went in the direction of a lady in her car, crying as she was trying to open a bottle. I tapped on the window and asked if I could help. She said, "I need to take my medication, but I can't get my bottle open." As I opened it for her, she commented that I was an answer to prayer. Then she graciously thanked me and took her medication. As I walked away, joy flooded my soul from being obedient to the Holy Spirit. Her cry for help was heard. Her prayer for help was answered.

Another steppingstone just happened.

CHAPTER 19
My mentor and friend is my divine appointment

I tried to leave home to go to the Giant supermarket at 7:30 AM. I had a full day planned, and adhering to the schedule was important. Somehow, I got sidetracked and by 8:30 AM, I was still reading and writing. It felt like I was missing opportunities to hand out gift cards at the grocery store. My personal devotional time this morning was so meaningful that I couldn't put it down. I've been trying to get a perspective of God's plan, instead of my plan. I've been trying to view life from heaven's point of view, instead of mine. What does God want to accomplish? What does God want me to do and when? How do I abandon my schedule and synchronize with God's? I was about to get schooled by the Holy Spirit. At 9:00 AM I got the nudge in my spirit that said, "Go now."

I dropped what I was doing, got in the truck, and headed for the shopping center. I had one prepaid card on my console. I put it in my back pocket and went inside the store, looking to give the card away. I could feel the anticipation, that today had a purpose. Little did I know!

Just around the corner, I heard someone say, "Hey you!" I couldn't believe my eyes! It was my mentor and friend, Paul Peterson from Western Pennsylvania. I couldn't help feeling overwhelmed with being "right on time!" It was so awesome to see him. God knew he was in town and arranged this encounter. Paul had encouraging words that I needed to hear. That's why he is my mentor. He claims that I had encouraging words for him, too. God cared enough to nudge me to go meet my friend. Just what I needed today.

A few years back, Paul Peterson was the appointed pastor at Victory Church, Columbia campus. He was the type of person who would be at the church at least one day a week so that he could prepare for the weekend. From time to time, I would notice his car there and would stop in and give him details of how God was using me. Paul would guide me in directions that made more sense than I was seeing. Almost on a weekly basis he would mentor me while being my friend. It came to a point where he felt the call to move back to Western Pennsylvania. When he left, it was a sad day for me. Many months went by without seeing him or talking to him, except for the occasional text. I was in tears when he showed up. He did not tell anybody he was in town, but God knew it and orchestrated it to bless us both.

CHAPTER 20
Divine appointments, timing is key

I wake up in the morning and say, God, what do you want from me today? Guide and direct me. With Parkinson's disease, I don't live a fast-paced life anymore. I am approaching the two-year mark since diagnosis. I still want to be used; I just don't have the dexterity. God has proved repeatedly that He can use me just the way I am. That is comforting!

After men's group and a time of prayer, I headed down to Columbia boat launch looking for homeless people. I looked around and didn't find anybody. I thought in my mind, I guess this time I missed what I felt the spirit was saying. I know in my heart that timing is key. Sometimes we must take a detour to be on time for our intended appointment. As I was descending Chickies Hill, I noticed a lady picking up cans and putting them in a bag. First, I thought she was part of a cleanup crew. Then I noticed the car she was driving. Suddenly in my heart I knew she was my divine appointment. I shrugged it off and kept driving. My heart pounding, I made a U-turn. She was just getting in her car as I pulled in behind her, but the traffic was so intense that she was not able to pull out. I tapped on her side window, and she opened it to talk to me. "Good morning," I started the conversation. We chatted a bit and I told her that I felt she was my appointment for today. She looked at me strangely and I said, "I feel like I should bless you today." I gave her a restaurant gift card and some cash. She was very thankful and proceeded to tell me that she makes ends meet by recycling cans. I thanked her for her service to the community with her cleanup efforts.

If we listen for that still small voice, we can be a blessing to those who need encouragement. She just needed to feel appreciated for what she does. Before I departed, I reminded her that she can always call on God, He's got your back. The look on her face . . .priceless!

So, I ask you, will you listen to that still small voice? Or do you not have time? People are crying out in many ways for help. Are you listening? Are you the answer that they need? You won't know until you act on what you hear and feel.

Fulfill the days that were written in your book. (Before you were born.)

Psalm 139:16 NLT

You saw me before I was born. Every day of my life was recorded in your book. Every moment was laid out before a single day had passed.

CHAPTER 21
Starting the fishing trip: Parkinson's Weary

New York state, Black Lake fishing trip. (chapters 21-23)

Every year I go on a fishing trip in May. I committed to do 28 days this year. I usually go with other guys for the first two weeks. Then as it warms up, Karen will come up for the final two weeks. At the last minute, several guys backed out. I now have time to do some reading, praying, writing, and resting. My only problem is I depend on other guys to help me with the boating, unpacking, and organizing the food, bedding, clothing, fishing supplies.

Just prior to going on my trip I felt that I really didn't want to go. I have not been doing well with Parkinson's. But I had given my word to several people in New York that I would be there. People that I only get to see once a year. I just had to press through the pain and keep my word.

As I was driving, just a few hours into my seven-hour trip, I was overwhelmed by not wanting to go any further, so I pulled over. I cried for God to give me the strength for this trip. I began to question God as to why Parkinson's is so hard. The tremor is so overwhelming. At times I just ask God to take me home and get it over with. At this time, I felt that I needed something tangible to get me through this trip. In the Bible, Gideon used a fleece. So, I said, "God if you would just give me one thing. I have a huge stye on my right eyelid. I've had it for over five years. It is irritating, annoying and still growing. God, if you could just remove it, I could rest in your promises for other things in my life. It would be enough for me to get through this trip."

I made it through the next four hours of driving. I arrived at a good time and unpacked. I washed my face, looking in the mirror at the stye on my eyelid. Thoroughly exhausted, I crashed early with the song "Gratitude" playing in the background. I woke up the next morning with a pasty feeling in my right eye. The stye burst overnight and was gone! Hallelujah! I can now look in the mirror and see God's handiwork every day! A constant reminder of his faithfulness. A reminder that His ways are higher than our ways.

Isaiah 55:8-9 NIV
For my thoughts are not your thoughts, Nor are your ways my ways," says the Lord. "For as the heavens are higher than the earth, So are my ways

higher than your ways, And my thoughts that your thoughts.

I can't wait to see what God is going to do on this trip. Let's start the adventure!

Here I am Lord, send (use) me!

CHAPTER 22
Lest I forget!

The weather is not cooperating. It is rainy and windy. I guess I'll write in my journal.

Lest I forget!

The scars. The five wounds comprised 1) the nail hole in His right hand, 2) the nail hole in His left hand, 3) the nail hole in His right foot, 4) the nail hole in His left foot, 5) the wound to His torso from the piercing of the spear.

Lest I forget!

The cross and its benefits. The shed blood for redemption. By His stripes we are healed. He was wounded for our transgressions. Our sin was nailed to the Cross.

Lest I forget!

The Father's heart: ask Me for the desires of your heart. Ask Me for the impossible. Ask Me for the things that seem out of reach and watch as I open doors that no person can close.

Psalm 37:4 ESV
Delight yourself in the Lord, and He will give you the desires of your heart.

Lest I forget!

The journey of life with its detours. Those detours are often what define us. Detours allow us to see the harsh side of life and remind us that God is ever present no matter where we are. There are even times He carries us through the detour.

Lest I forget!

The victories in life's battles. Not every battle is won. Help me to remember the sweet victories. Let the memories of the battles lost be a reminder that life is fragile, but the victory is won! We already know the end, and we are victorious!

Lest I forget!

The blessings of having children. Help me to remember the joys of parenting. Raising children and the fun we had in the process of learning and living.

Lest I forget!

Parents. Although my home was full of strife and tragedy, I still needed both parents to conceive me. Thank God, He wrote my name in the book and had a plan for me before I was formed in the womb. Help me to fulfill my purpose.

Lest I forget!

Lord God of Hosts, be with us, lest we forget! The concept of being careful not to forget was already present in the Bible.

Deuteronomy 4:9 NIV
Only be careful and watch yourselves closely so that you do not forget the things your eyes have seen or let them fade from your heart as long as you live. Teach them to your children and to their children after them.

CHAPTER 23
Having Church

Again, the weather is not cooperating for fishing, so I am reminiscing on a story that happened here in New York.

Thirteen years ago, I had an accident while towing my boat through New York. I had to have a friend, Albert Carter, bring his truck to load up all my things and tow the boat home. My truck was totaled. I felt bad that he came on a Sunday instead of going to church. I apologized to him for causing him to miss church. His reply was "Are you kidding? This is church!" The body of Christ helps each other. It's what we do!

That stuck with me for a long time! What a point he made.

So, the whole month of May I was in New York for some fishing, some God time, and having church! I stayed at a place called Fisherman's Landing. It's a small camp with six cabins about 50 feet from the water's edge. We typically stay in cabin #3. When I'm not fishing, my boat is tied up to the dock for the duration of the trip. The cabin rental is on a weekly basis. People are coming and going every weekend. I get to meet a lot of people and share my fishing expertise with them. I expect to see a lot of friends while I'm here because I've been coming up to this lake and meeting people for about 30 years.

During my stay I journaled about some examples of 'having church.'

May 12 early afternoon

I had an interesting day of ministry with an 84-year-old man whom I met here six years ago. I shared God's love with him. Little did I know that God was working in his heart at that time.

When I saw him on Friday, the first thing he said was, "I was hoping you would be here." I shared my current testimony with him, of my personal walk with God through Parkinson's disease. Then He shared that there were issues in his life that caused him to turn to God. Now, six years later, he is testifying of the goodness of God! We had a great time together. He is excited about the word of God. He shared his experience of Jesus being in the room while his wife was in the hospital for 48 days. Touch and go, and near death. He was in prayer every day until her recovery was complete. We cried together and hugged. I am so glad that God allowed me to be part of that.

Whether I'm catching fish or not, I am where I'm supposed to be: ministering to people, being the hands and feet of Jesus, having church daily.

May 12 afternoon

On Friday afternoon one of the fishermen in the neighboring cabin was having an issue with his boat trailer. He asked if I had any tools to fix it. I chuckled to myself and said, "of course." While someone was still praying, the answer was on the way. I love how God works. I had wrenches, bolts, screws, and an impact driver. While we had the tools out, we did a few other repairs. He wanted to pay me, but I declined. I told him God has your back. God provided the answer before you had the need. He thanked me again, loaded his boat, and went home. ("Here am I Lord, send me." Another steppingstone.)

May 13 afternoon
On Saturday, a new group of people came into camp. While launching the boat, they got a rope wrapped around the propeller. They were trying to remove the prop nut with an adjustable wrench. I asked the guy if there was anything they needed. "A lug socket and a breaker bar would be nice," he replied.

Again, I chuckled to myself, and said, "I have one of those." "Seriously?" he said in disbelief. "Yes, I'll go get it." The funny thing is, I almost removed it from my truck when I packed for this trip. It was right where it was supposed to be! Just when I needed it.

May 14 morning
It is now Sunday, and I was out fishing this morning. I knew I wanted to be done by 8:15 am so I could watch our church's service online. But something nudged me at

8 o'clock to go now! When I got to the dock, I tied up the boat. The guy next door was trying to start his boat, but the battery was dead. I offered some assistance, but he told me there was nothing I could do. They were disappointed because they were going for a Mother's Day boat ride. I went to my truck and got a jumper battery pack. I asked him if I could board the boat and start the motor. He reminded me that it was dead. "I know," I said, "But I can start it if you let me." He stepped aside and let me hook up the battery pack. He cranked and it started right up. They all thanked me, and I still had enough time to catch church online. "Being the church" is what we are called to do.

As church online was getting underway, I saw a small boat, fighting the wind wanting to get to the dock. I grabbed my extension pole and ran to their assistance. This was their first-time fighting the wind like that, and they had no clue how to navigate the wind while pulling into the dock. They were glad for my assistance. I tied up the boat, talked a bit and went back to my cabin. Once again, "having church" before church.

I have eight days of being alone here in New York before somebody comes up again to see me. I really battle being here alone. But I must be about my Father's business. I used to value alone time so I could go find new fishing spots. Now the alone time means I must watch my back. I get clumsy with Parkinson's. If somebody else was along I would be more comfortable. Especially going out in the dark at 3:00 AM.

Pastor Brett's message today really hit home. There are times that I wrestle with God over my struggle with Parkinson's disease. The tremor can be so debilitating. More and more I must trust God to sustain me. Pastor Brett said today that "God will give me everything I need, to do what I am called to do." I see that on a continual basis, like having a socket breaker bar, jumper pack, extension pole, impact screw gun, bolts and screws, fire extinguisher and other things that people need.

Opportunity is around every corner. Be willing to be an answer to someone's prayer. If we open our eyes, we will find it. Or it will find us! Are you ready to be the church? Exit your front door and enter the mission field. God is ready to answer someone's prayer using you!

May 22

God has been showing me the fruits of my labor these four weeks.

I was reunited on this trip with an older couple that I met ten years ago. Back then they had their son with them, an older teenager. He had no interest in doing good and was proud of being nasty. His anger was so intense. The cuss words just flowed from his mouth. You could hear him and his girlfriend verbally fighting when they were in the cabin. I felt horrified that a man would treat a woman that way. But he had such an interest in fishing. My first instinct was to take him out on the boat and show him how it's done. However, I did not allow him to have an attitude while on my boat.

I often wondered why he notched his eyebrows. I found out on this trip that ten years ago, his anger was so great, he would just punch someone and knock them out. Every eyebrow notch was for a knockout blow. I never felt threatened in his presence.

The report I got during this trip was that he is now the kindest, sweetest person you could ever want to meet. He is a great father. I asked them what it was that changed him? They replied, "You really don't know? You made the difference! For four years of vacationing here, you took him under your wings and showed him the value of life. You taught him how to fish. You showed him how to be a better person. That's what he needed. You showed him how to live life!"

So many times, I reach out, but never know the outcome. I'm not sure why God has allowed me to see so many results on this trip. With Parkinson's, I feel this could be my last trip to New York.

May 27 early morning

Upon rising I went to sit on the porch, looking out over the lake, having alone time with God. I felt overwhelmed with Parkinson's, but I surrendered to God's will for my life. This is what I heard Him say: "I know where you are because I have orchestrated the angels to go before you to make your paths straight. You are here in New York for a reason. Even though you are overwhelmed and feel like you shouldn't be here. There is a battle going on in the spiritual realm trying to stop you. This month I am showing you results from some of your ministries during your previous vacations here. You will not always see the results of everything you do. (Or should I say what "I AM" doing) I am showing you these things now, so that you can trust that I have your best interest at heart. It may not always be a pleasant or easy path. But I will give you strength. I will be your shield and defender. I will go before you, and I will be your rear guard. There is nothing that you will need that I haven't already provided. While you are in the middle of praying the answer is on the way."

Isaiah 65:24 NASB
It will also come to pass that before they call, I will answer; and while they are still speaking, I will hear.

May 27 mid-morning

For several days now it's been cold and windy. We had several weather patterns go through. God put somebody in my path to help me realize that it's not just about fishing. Enjoy life, enjoy the time you are here. Fulfill the days that God has assigned to you.

May 27 early afternoon

Another couple came into camp this week. "Hey John, do you remember us?" I didn't. "The last time we were here you told us about several spots that produced fish. We just weren't having a great time fishing until you came along. Thanks to you, we learned new areas to explore and learned how to catch fish. It was meaningful to us that you took the time to teach us."

While we were talking, he got a phone call. His buddy had shredded a tire on his boat trailer and was not going to be on time. After he got that tire changed, a few miles down the road, he blew another tire. Now he doesn't have another spare tire. I was listening to the conversation and felt I should tell him to look for Tractor Supply, because they have tires already on rims for trailers. There was one within six miles of where he was! When he got to Tractor Supply, the attendant told him of a guy who would come out with his wrecker, jack up the boat trailer, change the tires, and he would be on his way. He bought spare tires, and by the time he got back to the boat, the wrecker was already there to change the tires. I am so amazed at the intricacy of God. To have me standing where I needed to be, so that he would go to Tractor Supply. And at Tractor Supply he would find somebody to change the tire for him. How awesome is our God! Every little detail is known by Him and orchestrated by Him. God directs our steps.

Proverbs 3:5-6 NIV

Trust in the Lord with all your heart and lean not on your own understanding, in all your ways submit to Him, and He will make your paths straight.

May 27 evening

Today, I had two guys bring their boat right up to my dock and say "Hey, do you remember us?" I said, "tell me more." They said, "We were in the cabin next to you a couple of years ago. We were not catching fish, so you took the time to take us out on your boat and teach us how to look for them. You taught us all about structure and how to use the fishing lures effectively." I was so touched that they would look me up just to tell me that they appreciated it. I can't keep it to myself. We must testify what God has done for us, and how He uses us to touch others. Somebody out there needs to hear your testimony.

Revelation 12:11a NKJV
And they overcame him by the blood of the lamb, and the word of their testimony.

May 29 morning
My Memorial Day tributes.
To all those who fought the good fight: thank you for your service to our country. For those who never made it home, we are eternally grateful for your sacrifice.

We are at war! Believers must understand that "this war for souls" has eternal consequences.

What do I need to do to be used by God to fight the spiritual battle and rescue those perishing around me? We are at war, and we must be diligent to advance the kingdom of Christ.

Somewhere in a sermon I heard the following story.

A young football coach was hired as a scout for his college. Before his first assignment, he said, "Coach, what kind of player are you looking for?" The coach said, "well there's a kind of guy that when you knock him down, he just stays down." The recruiter asked, "we don't want him, do we, Coach?" "No!" Then the coach said to the recruiter. "There's a kind of guy who when you knock him down, he gets up and he keeps getting up, repeatedly." "That's the guy we want! Right, Coach?" "No, we don't want him either. What I want you to find is the guy who keeps knocking all the other guys down. That's the guy I want!"

Will you be that person who will speak the truth to strangers no matter what? Will you be the one who tears down walls and sets people free? Remember, their eternal destiny depends on it.

Ezekiel 3:18 NKJV

When I say to the wicked, 'You shall surely die,' and you give him no warning, nor speak to warn the wicked from his wicked way, to save his life, that same wicked man shall die in his iniquity; but his blood I will require at your hand.

May 29 pm

By now, I'm really enjoying the presence of God on this trip. I'm getting to write about the great things that God has been doing, even in the little things.

There was another guy in camp this week. He was having electrical issues. Long story short, there were problems with the battery. While I was looking at the charging system, I found a problem. But in between a lot of his cuss words, he happened to say, "thank God."

I replied, "yes, Amen, I thank him every day." He was stunned but said amen to that. God has a way of using situations to give you an "in" so that you can share testimonies with someone. Let your test be your testimony for others. The electrical problems persisted throughout the week. Again and again, I was able to show favor to this man. I have no clue what God will do with these moments. But with all that I have seen, I really don't have to know, trusting in God to make a great outcome.

June 1 end of trip

Throughout my time here, I was able to share past stories of answered prayer. I believe that our testimonies of answered prayer strengthens us and others. Here are two stories that I shared.

During my construction career, I had an encounter with a Russian Christian/non-believer. In other words, he said he was a Christian, but he had no personal relationship with Jesus. I asked him what made him a Christian. He said in his Russian accent, "I live in America, that makes me a Christian." I chuckled and said OK. We were getting ready to leave the job site to head back to the shop for the weekend. The truck would not start. The battery was dead. He tried everything he could to get it running. The foreman on the job was getting very agitated because it was Friday, and he just wanted to get home. I suggested that we lay hands on the battery and pray for it. "Are you nuts?!" he replied.

I commented, "You did everything else, but not that." As I was praying, I told him to get into the truck and try again. The Russian guy said it's no use. But then I said, "what do you have to lose?" The foreman got into the truck, and with prayers answered, the truck started. The Russian guy chuckled and said there must've been some juice in there after all. I knew better! God was having a moment in both their lives.

I had another incident where a rainstorm was coming. It hit us about the time church service was over. I had about an hour to drive in the rain to get to my destination. The windshield wipers would not work! We prayed for it, but it did not work. I went back to the church to talk to the pastor and asked for his advice. He said, "Well, of course lay hands on it and pray for it, and if that doesn't work, lay a hammer to it!" So, I did what I was told. I laid hands on it again and prayed. It did not work. I grabbed a hammer and hit the motor housing. It worked! I was only following instructions. To what extent will you go to get your prayers answered? Would you do something that sounds stupid? Within reason, of course. I wouldn't want you to do something unlawful or illegal.

2 Kings 5:13-14 NLT

But his officers tried to reason with him and said, "Sir, if the prophet had told you to do something very difficult, wouldn't you have done it? So you should certainly obey him when he says simply, 'go

and wash and be cured!'" So Naman went down to the Jordan river and dipped himself seven times, as the man of God had instructed him. And his skin became as healthy as the skin of a young child, and he was healed!

June 2
Going home is bittersweet!
Saying goodbye until next year.

Dear God, thank you for Your generosity. Thank You for going before me, to clear the way, and for being my rearguard! Thanks for being my best friend. Love, John

CHAPTER 24
The approach, going the extra mile

I remember the time I was at a gas station filling my truck. A young lady came walking towards me with a scowl on her face. "Hey sir, can you spare five dollars for some gas? My gas tank is empty, and I can't find anybody who's willing to help me." Immediately I felt her desperation. I didn't want to compound the bad feelings. "Of course I will. Which car is yours?" She pointed to an older beat-up car, not even at the pumps yet. I told her to pull it up and I will fill it up. The tears started to flow. "You have no idea what this means." I replied, "I think I do."

The Bible says if anybody asks for your shirt, give them your coat also. She only wanted $5. I used my credit card to fill up her car, and then I gave her the cash in my pocket. I'm at a point in life where I don't have to know why. If she has a need for gas, she has a need for other things as well.

I started to think about everybody who missed an opportunity. Were they so busy judging her that they didn't give anything to her? Sometimes it's better not to think it through. Just respond. And yes, every now and then, but not often, I feel bad after I've given to somebody. I think giving is about obedience more than a feeling afterwards. I can't totally put my finger on it, but I choose to give anyway. And if somebody misuses the funds that I give, God will be the judge. The Bible says that if somebody has hurt or offended us, God will be their judge. It's not up to us to do that!

1 Peter 4:19b NIV
Continue to do good.

Matthew 5:42 NLT
Give to those who ask, and don't turn away from those who want to borrow.

CHAPTER 25
The approach, addressing fears and insecurities

It still happens to me today. I find great opposition in my head when I am approaching someone that God wants me to bless. My heart will practically jump out of my chest, and I just want to walk away. I am telling you to persevere! Let God use you.

Keep in mind:

a) Always approach with humility.

b) Find common ground to start the conversation.

c) Know what you believe in your heart before you start. Create your own list.

Here is my list:

I believe....

1. The Bible is the inspired word of God.

2. All truth must line up with the word of God.

3. All people are created in God's image and deserve respect.

4. We are all the hands and feet of Jesus.

5. Our passion and purpose are given to us by our Creator.

This is what I want people to know as I approach them. It must show in my body language as well as my words. If I choose to minister to you, I want you to know through my actions that I respect what you believe, and I respect you as a person. I may not agree with what you believe, and I am not here to judge or argue. Arguing does not lead to salvation or peace. I might invite you along on my journey and give you gift cards to give away. My goal is to be salt and light in your world.

I feel that when I approach somebody it doesn't have to have a verbal sermon attached to it. My actions are the sermon! I have learned over the years that God will give you a way into their sphere to help, rather than intrude. You will see in my stories that something happens to give me a chance to help others. The Bible talks about the good Samaritan. Are you one? Or do you pass by when somebody needs help? Are you looking for opportunities?

The parable of the Good Samaritan is told by Jesus in the Gospel of Luke. (10:25-37) It is about a traveler who is stripped of clothing, beaten, and left half dead alongside the road. First, a Jewish priest and then a Levite come by, but both avoid the man. Finally, a Samaritan happens upon the traveler.

Luke 10:33 NLT

Then a despised Samaritan came along, and when he saw the man, he felt compassion for him.

A despised and hated Samaritan was the hero. Now go and do the same.

Jesus said, "Love one another."

How you are loving your neighbor will prove to the world that you are my disciples. There is no loophole! We are commanded to love. How are you impacting the kingdom of God?

Question:

Is it a divine appointment or just being a good Samaritan?

Was the account with the good Samaritan in the Bible a divine appointment or just an illustration of being a person who does good for others? You don't always have to have a divine appointment to do good for others!

CHAPTER 26
Sometimes it's complicated!

My day started off like this: after a mid-morning appointment, I drove around thinking about who I could minister to today. I ended up in the parking lot of a grocery store. Usually when that happens, I buy gift cards to give away. I only bought two today. It didn't take long to give them away. People are hurting financially. I am more than happy to help young families put food on their table.

A young mother with three toddlers was an easy assumption. I told her I had a question for her. She was all ears, despite the people cutting between us. She was patient to hear what I had to say. I asked how the food prices affect her family. I did not know if there were more children than the three that were with her. Through her smile she admitted that it was tough, but they managed somehow. I offered her a $50 gift card that she could use at the register. Her eyes lit up. She was thankful, with tears flowing. Then we talked for a while. Sometimes conversations get personal. We wiped away the tears and moved on.

I saw a young man carrying his baby while filling the baby stroller with food. I chuckled. I approached him and asked if he could use $50 towards today's purchase? "No way, are you kidding?" Then he said, "you can't be serious!" I replied, "yes way! I am serious.' He said he could definitely use it. He gave me a hug, graced me with some small talk, and then departed.

I really enjoyed my time at the grocery store. But now it was time to go. The next leg of my journey was complicated. Sometimes things don't make sense. I was at a loss today. I did what I thought I was supposed to do. Then I started to question myself. Was I not in tune to hear God? Or was I just not hearing anything?

I came home saddened by today's third encounter. I could do nothing for the man, nor do I think he wanted anything done. I had to really pray about this one. Here is what happened: I picked up a pizza and headed to the park where the homeless hung out. I never know what to expect. Taking food with me gives me an "in" so I can talk to them. I started approaching a man sitting in the shade. I noticed he was wearing an eyepatch. Trying not to startle him, I announced my position. He said, "yeah, I heard you coming. I'm blind in one eye, and only have 5% vision in the other." The man talked a mile a minute about everything and nothing. From his ramblings, I gathered that he was a war veteran and had brain damage from improvised explosive devices that he encountered in war. He said he could not accept the pizza that I was offering because it would violate his code of ethics even though he hadn't eaten in three days. He knew it was foolishness on his part and admitted it. But unless he could pay for it, he wasn't going to eat it. I sat the pizza beside him and said, "You can eat it, or let it go to waste." He said, "hold on a minute." He pulled a carpenter tool out of his pocket and said, "I want you to have this." I replied, "I can't take it from you." He then said, "if the cops stop me, it will be considered a weapon. Please take it," so I took it. He replied, "Thanks. Now I paid for the pizza."

Many thoughts raced through my head. I never had such an encounter before. The man obviously was gripped with anguish from the tragedy of the explosions. I wanted to pray with him, I wanted to console him. He wanted nothing of either. I was baffled. I had answered a lot of his questions, not knowing what the answers meant to him. But as I left, he made a final statement. "Sir, you truly are a man of God. In all my years, I've never met anyone like you." I kept on walking. I did not know how to respond. I felt helpless as I got in my truck and drove away. Holy Spirit, you take it from here.

CHAPTER 27
Choose to give

Yesterday I sent a text to the Mount Joy Food Bank to see what they needed. This morning the text read: We need jelly! We have a vast amount of peanut butter, but no jelly. Opportunity presented itself. I love to give. I headed to the bargain outlet. I loaded my cart with different flavors and sizes of jelly, and some honey, apple butter, and marshmallow fluff. I want more than jelly with my peanut butter! The cashier rang it up and I loaded my truck. I got to the food bank about 30 minutes before they opened. I felt great about meeting the need. I dropped it off quickly and made my exit. The feeling I get from giving is beyond description. As I drove off, I was in a generous mood. Not everything I do is heavenly directed. Sometimes I just "choose to give," but I guess that is scriptural too.

Luke 6:35 ESV
But love your enemies, and do good, and lend, expecting nothing in return, and your reward will be great.

The true reward of being good to others is that we get to spread some joy.

I went to Giant with the intention of giving away four gift cards. I paid for the cards and my groceries. I proceeded through the store looking for somebody to bless. I spotted a man with an infant and asked him how he was doing. He said he was good, so find somebody who really needs it. My second prospect said the same thing, but she was excited that somebody was willing to be kind to others.

I kept looking until I found somebody who could use it. An elderly lady accepted my card with sincere thanks and knew immediately that this was a God thing. She asked me questions about my church, so we talked for a while.

Then as I continued down the aisle, I saw a man with a huge cart of food with large quantities of the same items. I was curious. As I started to talk to him, I noticed his name tag read "Rick" and "HOSPICE." I've given items to our local hospice numerous times. I told him that I give to the organization from time to time and offered him a $50 gift card. He accepted it and we talked for fifteen minutes about his topics. We shook hands and moved on.

Two gift cards down, two to go. Another lady passed around my back, not wanting to go between me and the guy I was just talking to. I stopped her and questioned her on how she's handling the prices. "What can I do?" she asked. "I buy what I can and that's it." I saw the coupons in her hand and offered her a gift card. She asked, "why me?" I said I think you're doing a great job using coupons and I want to offer it to you. Her face lit up. She thanked me and then continued shopping.

As I turned around, there was another gentleman standing there with coupons in his cart. I don't know if he heard me or the conversation that just happened. But I offered him a card as well. His reply was, "you don't have to do that." I asked him, "so you're telling me you can't use it?" "Oh, I can use it. My wife has health issues, she is sitting in the car because she can't follow me through the store." He asked me questions about my church and told me about his. Then he told me his son is a pastor upstate. He was glad for a story that he could share with his son. "There are still good people out there," he said. I agreed.

There are times I listen for God's voice to specifically direct me to someone in need. And there are times I just go looking for it!

Proverbs 19:17 NIV
Whoever is kind to the poor lends to the Lord, and he will reward them for what they have done.

CHAPTER 28
Gold, no Plan B

My wife had some gold jewelry that was not being used. We decided to cash it in for ministry purposes. The place I chose was not open this morning. So, I went home to work on a project. I had no Plan B in place. Around 3:00 PM it hit me: I had not sold the gold yet. I figured I would just find a place close to home. Suddenly, I knew where to go, and it was just a few minutes from home. I was greeted quickly by Marcie, and soon our conversation went all over the world! We talked about everything from remodeling my house to my mission trips in Brazil and Honduras. Then she talked about her experience with feeding the hungry and homeless. I chuckled as I told her my plans for the cash from the jewelry: "I plan to use it in ministry to feed people."

She handed me the check and said, "I just want you to know something. I was having a really bad morning until you came along! Thanks for lifting my mood. You have no idea how you blessed me."

I really didn't know. I was just being me. I was in the right place at the right time. God's timing! I was just being obedient, and God cared enough for her that He sent me to bless her.

Matthew 6:8b NIV
Your Father knows what you need before you ask Him.

You don't decide who you are, you discover who you are. Your assignment is geographical. You don't belong everywhere, but you belong somewhere.

Where you are matters as much as who you are. You are not important to everybody. You won't be missed by many! How do you know who you are assigned to? Whose pain do you feel? Whose success consumes you? What occupies your thought life? You were designed with a purpose for a purpose.

CHAPTER 29
Is it starting to make sense?

Are you getting the idea? Are you starting to hear the little things that God is saying to you? Are you finding your purpose?

As you continue reading, you will see that most of the things that I am called to do are similar, like handing out gift cards. However, God will throw something different my way to see if I am listening. One day I might start out driving eastbound and make a right turn; the next day I might go north and turn left. This usually means that I have a specific assignment for a divine appointment. When I'm not hearing anything, and I just want to be a blessing, I frequent the same stores because of the geographical area that I am called to. As you glance around, people are in need. There is hurt everywhere you look in your community, in your town, and in your county. Start where you live and walk through your neighborhood. Talk to people. Hear what they are saying. When you go for groceries or gas, to work or church, God knows where you will be before you get there. He can orchestrate an answer to somebody's prayer before you leave the house. He needs willing vessels! Surrender your day to Him, and He will do the rest. All He requires is your obedience.

Eph 5:17 GNT

Make good use of every opportunity you have because the days are evil.

CHAPTER 30
On time again!

Proverbs 3:5-6 NLT
Trust in the LORD with all your heart; do not depend on your own understanding.
Seek his will in all you do, and he will show you which path to take.

I was wrestling with timing as I started my day. I had a game plan in place, but I was uncertain about the timing. I wanted to leave but I felt held back. Over an hour later, I finally walked out the door. I was going to go get tools from my storage unit. I figured ten minutes tops, and I would be gone. I was loaded and ready to leave when a garbage truck blocked the entrance of the parking lot. I sat there for five minutes. They did not move or attempt to take any garbage. They were just talking to each other. Just as I was getting ready to ask them to move, I recognized one of the workers. He picks up our residential trash during the week. Typically, twice a year I bless our guys with restaurant gift cards in appreciation for their service. Having a few extra cards in the truck serves me well. I grabbed them and went to him. He thought it was so cool that I remembered who he was. He thanked me for the card, moved the truck, and I was on my way.

I arrived at my scheduled appointment 45 minutes early! They took me in right away because the first appointment did not show up. This was critical for my next divine appointment. It was not on my schedule. But now that I was done early, I headed towards Columbia. I felt that I was to park in the Giant parking lot and wait. OK, I thought, I will just wait for directions from God. I still had a $50 gift card from the last time I was at Giant, so there was no need to go inside to get any.

As I was waiting, I spotted a young lady with an infant. She had a sweatshirt on that said, "live generously." I was about to fulfill that very thought. She had just finished putting the groceries in the car as I approached her. "I like your T-shirt logo! Our church has one that says, 'make a difference.' I would like to bless you with a gift card for Giant." She thought that was so awesome. I said, "I enjoy helping young families as they face what life throws at them."

Her final statement was, "make sure that you tell your pastor that this really works. I appreciate that you are handing out gift cards and making a difference."

One thing to remember: God's timing is awesome. I should have been at the chiropractor instead of being here blessing her. Orchestrated or coincidence? You decide, but I believe it was God's timing!

CHAPTER 31
Impeccable timing again!

I tried to leave home around 7 am this morning. I finally left around 9:30 am. Just a few minutes down the road, traffic was almost at a standstill. When my schedule is interrupted, like a traffic delay, I often wonder what God is up to. Does he have something for me that requires timing? When I finally got to Home Depot, I sat in the truck for a few minutes to gather my thoughts, checking my list for what I wanted to buy. As I looked up, I thought, no, it couldn't be! It was my friend Tom from church. I was surprised to see him at the Lancaster store when he normally buys from the York store. I was able to flag him down before he pulled away. He had been in Alaska for a few weeks over the summer. He said that he was purchasing gift cards for his nephew. Tom recently did a mission trip to the homestead in Alaska where his nephew lives. The gift cards will help buy supplies needed to expand. I offered up a gift card that I was holding on to for a future purchase. What a surprise for both of us! He can now send an extra gift card for the family. Another opportunity, another blessing, perfect timing.

Luke 6:38 NKJV

Give, and it will be given to you: good measure, pressed down, shaken together, and running over will be put into your bosom. For with the same measure that you use, it will be measured back to you.

CHAPTER 32
Complaining is to the devil, what praise is to the Lord.

It all depends on where your eyes are focused. When I look at modern day America, I see we have so many conveniences. Climate controlled houses. Luxury vehicles to transport us. Internet and cell phones. Jets to take us around the world in one day. We have the convenience of eating food from just about anywhere in the world. We live better today than most kings did 100 years ago. So, what is your problem? Why all the complaining? Why do you live in the past? Jesus raised you up and seated you in heavenly places, He gave you all authority in heaven and earth. If you have all the authority, who has no authority? Just think about it. If I have all the pie, that means somebody has no pie. The enemy does not have authority unless we give it to him. Jesus gave us all the authority. Jesus said, "Do not leave here until you have received the Holy Spirit. Then you will be endued with power." Satan has been disarmed and defeated at the cross.

The giants in your life are not meant to destroy you, they are meant to reveal you. When David was up against Goliath, it was so God could reveal who David was. He was anointed before he was appointed. Defeating the giant, God showed who David really was. Now was his appointed time.

I'm starting to see that having Parkinson's disease was a giant set before me to show me who I am in Christ. Parkinson's was not meant to defeat me, but to reveal to me and others who I am.

Romans 8:28 NIV
And we know that in all things God works for the good of those who love him, who have been called according to his purpose.

CHAPTER 33
Overflow of kindness sweeps through marriage

I was in Leola today and felt impressed to stop at the park. Just as I arrived, I got a 30-minute phone call from a friend who wanted to talk about the health benefits of good eating. I had a great conversation and was glad I was parked while I was talking. I don't like to talk and drive.

During the conversation, a young couple pulled in beside me and took their toddler to the playground. I watched as I saw what I thought was the couple arguing over something. The wife came back to the car and looked very distraught. I was praying for them and talking on the phone at the same time. It's my effort to pray without ceasing.

She returned to her husband and shortly thereafter, they all came back to the car to leave. I just finished my phone call. I lowered my window and asked what they were doing for lunch. "Nothing out of the ordinary," they replied.

I said, "I would like to buy you lunch if you could tell me where you would like to go?" They asked about their options. I pulled out a stack of gift cards for restaurants. I told them I had a variety from McDonald's and Burger King to Olive Garden and steak houses. With tears, the wife said that her daughter wanted McNuggets for lunch and she had to tell her no. They accepted the McDonald's card and asked why I did this. I said, "I've been where you are. Young and struggling from time to time while trying to raise a family. This is our way to give back and help firm your foundation."

As I left, I saw them embracing and crying. Now they're making me cry. Who will you affect today?

God's challenge to us:

I don't want you to just memorize My Word, I want you to become My Word. I want you to be my hands and feet. I haven't called you just to go to church, I called you to be the church! Open your eyes and learn to see what I see.

Wow, I thought. Mercy got me out of bed and gave me another chance to be like Him! He anoints my head, my cup runs over, then it spills out into the world and affects everybody it reaches.

CHAPTER 34
Something different today

Some days I just enjoy being generous, however, today was a divine appointment! God had an agenda.

As I was writing down my goals for today, I realized I did not cash three checks yesterday. I had to make plans to go to the bank. This particular incident set perfect timing in motion for the day. Had I done this the day before it would've messed up the timing of a divine appointment, as you will see later. My goal was to be at a specific church by 11:00 am. Several traffic delays and a missed event sent my schedule into orbit. You would think that I would know by now: God's timing is better than mine. As I was driving towards the bank, I knew in my heart I was to cash the checks and give the money away. I requested one big bill, folded it, and placed it in an envelope. As I was driving down the road, God told me where, when, and why. I will leave out names for privacy purposes.

I heard about a young man who just started as an assistant pastor. From a previous experience in my life, I knew how that could go awry. I served under the pastor in a city church when I was in my early 20s. My visions of what I thought would happen as an assistant to the pastor never materialized. The pastor had expectations of me that he never expressed. That led to a crumbling situation. When we realized that his terms were non-negotiable, we gave our notice and moved home. I fully respect the man and what he accomplished during his 40-year tenure since then. Not everybody is compatible. Even the apostle Paul had issues working with some other people. During my stay, I met a lot of good people and had a lot of great experiences. This is the church I attended when I met the Russian guy that I previously talked about. I would not trade this adventure for anything. It was definitely a pruning and growing experience.

God told me to hand this young assistant pastor the envelope and tell him that I believe in him, and I am sowing seed into his ministry. I was to affirm that his assignment may not make sense at times, but he should continue to be obedient to the call. As you grow, God will use people to reward you with gifts and finances. Be gracious and humble when you receive and don't turn down any gift, great or small. God will use the heart of people to affirm your calling. The things that don't make sense will be the very things that create your steppingstones. Trust those steppingstones as God directs your path.

I thought to myself, wow, God that's a lot to remember. But I trust that You will bring to my remembrance the things that You want to be said to this assistant pastor.

I arrived at my destination, feeling like I was thirty minutes late, but with confidence that I was on time. I walked into the church office and was directed to where a meeting was just ending. As I stood outside the room, I heard these words "in Jesus' name, amen." The meeting was over. I was right on time! God's time.

I introduced myself, handed the assistant pastor the envelope with the cash, and told him about what happened to me early in my life. He gave me that look, you know, the look when somebody just read your mail! He proceeded to tell me the challenges that he was up against as an assistant pastor. He then thanked me for sowing seed into his ministry and for the encouraging words. We hugged, we prayed, we cried, and I departed with a satisfaction that goes beyond what words can describe.

A well-known pastor named Brett Rush recently said, "At the end of the day it's not about how much harvest you've reaped, it's about how much seed you've sown."

Matthew 6:10 NKJV
Your Kingdom come, your will be done on earth as it is in heaven.

It is all about God's purpose! Before you were born, your purpose was written in your book. It's up to you to fulfill it.

A person often meets their destiny on the very road that they took to avoid it.

God bless the broken roads that lead to the best destinations!

CHAPTER 35
Blessing the Mount Joy Food Bank

My truck was loaded with food and ready to deliver. I had to make this quick because I had a 9 am appointment. I try to get to the food bank before they open so they have time to sort the items that I bring. I briefly talked to the volunteers, and they thanked me for the donations. All glory to God and our new Mount Joy church campus. We are getting established within the community and making a difference.

As I left the food bank, I passed a mail truck picking up mail from a collection box. I felt the need to give her a gift card and thank her for her service, but I thought, maybe another time, I must be somewhere soon. I got about two blocks away and it hit me hard. I knew I had to turn around and attempt to find her. I found the truck parked at another collection box, so I pulled in front of it. I approached her, introduced myself, and told her I would like to buy her lunch. Her name was Kaylee. She was taken aback, and said, "excuse me? Say what?"

I answered her, "it's what I do, I find people to bless. My goal is to make a difference. While doing so, I get to meet new people and make new friends." I told her I was sorry that I only had McDonald's cards. I normally have a better variety. Kaylee said, "McDonald's is just fine, I eat there! You just made my day. It's awesome to see what you do." We laughed for a few minutes, then I let her get back to work.

Would you rather do nothing, or make them laugh? We do have a choice, you know. I choose to change the atmosphere in a positive way.

Make a difference!

CHAPTER 36
Position yourself to be a blessing

I was in Columbia and Wrightsville this morning taking pictures around sunrise. I had about twenty minutes before I had to leave for my next appointment, so I positioned my truck in a space outside the grocery store. Just sitting there, 10 minutes went by, and nothing happened. Maybe I missed it? Give it a little time.

A lady in her early 40s walked by. I knew at that moment that she was in need. I grabbed a gift card and entered the store. By the time I found her, she had a few items in her cart. I asked if she could use some help paying for her purchase today. She hesitated but answered, "yes." Then I slipped her a gift card. She sobbed and said it couldn't have come at a better time. Her daughter was coming home from college today, and she had no food for her. She thanked me, gave me a hug, and reminded me how timely it was. She told me her name, I told her mine, and I said, "Have a blessed day!" And I went on my way.

Do you purposely position yourself to be a blessing? Are you looking for an opportunity? Are you sensing what the Holy Spirit is saying? Do you listen to His voice like, "stop here and wait?" Both eyes open, looking all around, what do you see? What do you hear? What do you feel? You are in training!

CHAPTER 37
Teach someone else how to make a difference

I had one grocery card on me and did not have the time to purchase another one. I walked into the store with the intent of quickly giving it away. I saw a toddler standing in the cart, giggling, and rubbing noses with his mother. I commented, "how cute is that!" We all had a good laugh at this Hallmark moment. "I think you deserve a prize for that. How about a gift card towards your purchase today?"

She thought about it for a moment and replied, "I would feel guilty taking it from you. Certainly, somebody else needs it more than I do. I appreciate that you offered it to me, and it is something that I would like to do someday."

I hesitated in responding, listening for the Holy Spirit to guide me. Then I asked, "what if I were to give it to you, for you to give it to someone else?" She came back quickly. "Yes, that sounds good, I can do that!" She eagerly took the card and thanked me. I was now thinking that is a win, win! I get to give it to who I intended it for, and she gets to experience the joy of giving it to someone who needs it. Priceless! I looked back. The smile was still on her face as she told her story to the cashier.

My job here is done.

Each one teach one!

2 Timothy 2:2

You have heard me teach things that have been confirmed by many reliable witnesses. Now teach these truths to other trustworthy people who will be able to pass them on to others.

CHAPTER 38
Start the day with prayer

Then what? Are you ready to enter the mission field? Our men's group gathered at 7:00 am for a time of reviewing Sunday's message about marriage and then praying about how we can change for the better. Raw honesty! No judgment! Iron sharpening iron.

After the men's group was over, I decided to go to Dollar Tree for more supplies for the Mount Joy Food Bank. After I paid for my items, I offered to pay for the young lady next in line. She smiled and said, "you may, only if you want to!"

"Oh, I want to," I replied. I paid with cash and gave her the money that I received in return.

Her comment was, "it is so good to see generosity instead of meanness." We had fun talking for a moment, then I loaded my things for the food bank.

I normally donate to the food bank once a month. I did not understand why I did it twice this week, until I was done. Then it was clear that God was leading. One of the volunteers was missing on Wednesday but was present today. He told me he had to take his wife to the hospital on Wednesday with heart issues. I agreed to put her on our prayer list. He needed to know someone cared enough to ask. I have asked him questions in the past, when dropping off donations. I knew Burger King was one of his favorite places to eat. I gave him a gift card so he could get lunch before going to the hospital to see his wife. I could see the look on his face. He was grateful for the card but was concerned for his wife. That's quite a load to carry on your own. We need each other.

Be prepared! I try to be stocked with a variety of gift cards for gas, restaurants, and grocery stores. A gift card can create an opening to minister, just one of many tools in the toolbox!

There are many ways to minister to people, to show that you care, with or without finances. I have shown you ways that work for me. For you, it could be different. Just talking, listening, or offering to pray. Do what works for you! God wants to use you! Tell Him that you volunteer!

CHAPTER 39
Living out the written Word of God

I enjoy it when my wife cooks new things. Today she was experimenting with a new recipe. However, she did not have all the ingredients. I needed to go to the grocery store for one item. Without hesitation, I grabbed two grocery cards and went into the grocery store. It was packed! It was hard to find a cart because the store was full of people. Anyway, I grabbed the item I needed and paid for it. As I turned around, I saw a lady with a very full cart. I commented on the full cart and asked her if she could use some help paying for her groceries today. She said, "of course." She was so surprised when I handed her a gift card. I noticed that she was holding up the line, so I did not say much more except, "you have a blessed day!"

I walked out the door and headed towards my truck. I saw another lady with many empty bags coming into the store. She hesitated, looking for a cart. I approached her and asked if she could use some help paying for her groceries today. "Yes," she said bluntly. I handed her a card and said, "you have a blessed day," and then I walked away.

It was like they never knew what hit them! Random acts of kindness. Like the commercial says, "What's in your wallet?" What random act of kindness will you commit today?

CHAPTER 40
A Day of many opportunities

I woke up around 4 o'clock this morning. The moon was bright. It was a full moon as well, a good photo opportunity at the river in Columbia. I headed to the boat ramp to watch the moon set over the west shore. I talked to fishermen as well as a photographer. We got some good shots of the moon setting. The photographer told me he lived in Columbia all his life. I asked him which church he grew up in. Trinity Lutheran. His wife went to parochial school there as a child. Having a base line of church knowledge gave me the opportunity to talk about God. I'm finding new ways to steer the conversation in a spiritual direction.

After taking about 100 photos, I packed up my equipment and headed to the west shore in Wrightsville. Once the sun starts coming out, many people show up to take photographs. I talked to a local who lived up on the hill. We did not discuss much in the realm of Godly things, but we got enough of a base that I got his name, and he got mine. See you here again?

The view was just awesome. As I was photographing the bridge, a lady came beside me and said, "excuse me, can I share your view?"

"Absolutely!" I said while laughing at her comment.

She was from New York. Gretchen said her husband Jim was in their motorhome parked at the top of the hill. She also said they recently retired and started traveling. She wanted to know where they could take in a good view. I directed them to a state park up on the hill. Gretchen asked me what I did with my pictures. That opened the door!

"I take my pictures and put scriptures on them and send them out to people to encourage them."

"Well, that's just awesome!" she responded. I asked her about her husband Jim. Gretchen said they decided to travel while they can, due to his health condition. He had to retire because he had a stroke, but he has recovered. They also discovered he has diabetes. I assured her that I would pray for him. She was grateful.

As I was getting ready to leave, there was a boat in the parking lot. I recognized the guy from the Susquehanna Fishing Tackle store. His name is Mike. He noticed my tremor and asked about it. I told him about the last two years with Parkinson's. I told him I can only last about three hours fishing before I wear out. He said it's about the same with him, but he has Myeloma. Another open door and ministry opportunity. They were about to go fishing. I showed them a few spots that they could try. Sadly, I learned that five months later, Mike lost his battle with Myeloma. He was active in his community and will be missed.

I prayed for several people this morning. God opened doors to let me minister. As I moved from one person to another, I was praying for them in the spirit. God knows what they need.

Romans 8:18 NKJV
Likewise the spirit also helps in our weaknesses. For we do not know what we should pray for as we ought, but the Spirit Himself makes intercession for us with groanings which cannot be uttered.

I sent a text to a friend of mine. I sent him some pictures and encouragement for his day. So many people are hurting. So many people have health issues.

That was just the start of my day. I also had an opportunity to jumpstart a car for our friend Carol and buy her a new battery. She attends Victory Church, Mount Joy campus with us. I talked to her for about 20 minutes, which was necessary for my next encounter to happen. If I did not talk that amount of time, I would have missed another great opportunity on my way home. I saw somebody along the road who ran out of gas. It happened two minutes before I arrived. If I did not talk as long as I did, I would've been home by now, missing this opportunity. I told him I live around the corner, hang tight. I went home and got my gas cans. He was from New Jersey. He started the car, gave me a fist bump, and was on his way. He had offered me some money, but I would not take it. He could not understand why. I said, "I just want to bless you." He said, "indeed I am."

Psalms 32:8 CEV
God, you said to me, "I will point out the road that you should follow. I will be your teacher and watch over you."

God's timing! So awesome. As I walked in the door, my wife said, "are you done with Divine appointments?" I said, "for now."

So many opportunities. Are we looking for them, or do we just drive by?

CHAPTER 41
Saying goodbye

Victory Church Columbia Campus was having a send-off party for Pastor Josh and Jaclyn. They were leaving for their new adventure at Caring Place Church in Indiana.

We were about 30 minutes into the party when I felt a nudge to go minister. They were starting to set up chairs for the extra people. It was a good time to sneak out. We had already said our goodbyes. We heard great testimonies about Pastor Josh and Jaclyn before we left. We are aware of their impact on this community.

Karen and I got in the truck and headed towards Wrightsville to the location where I prayed for a couple from New York. I thought maybe I would see them again. God had other things in mind. We met Gina, the lady who rented the space to the campers from New York. She told us the story from Gretchen, the lady I met on Saturday morning. Gina was so astonished at the things she said of our meeting at the river, how I shared scriptures, and how I prayed for her family. Gretchen was also impressed at how I get around to minister to people since having

Parkinson's. I told her that I go where I am called. God tells me to go, and I go. I start driving and listening.

Gina told us that God pulled her out of a troubled life when she was younger. Now she's hearing about God's greatness through other people. Her eyes light up when we talk about God's love, grace, and His timing. We were there for almost an hour, testifying of God's greatness.

Revelation 12:11a NKJV
And they overcame him by the blood of the lamb, and the word of their testimony.

CHAPTER 42
What if . . .you tell me!

I am wondering what my encounter will be today. Will this be the day that I am healed? Will this be another day that I get to minister to someone's needs?

Today is Saturday. I get to do some maintenance work at Karen's place of business. Saturday is the only day I can get things done without employees or technicians being in my way. About 2-1/2 hours into my project, I needed some electrical supplies that I did not have. So, I wrapped it up for today and headed home. I noticed a gift card laying on my console and thought about possibly giving it away. I just missed the exit for the grocery store. I figured I'd just do it another time. But what if I was supposed to be there? But what if someone was praying for help and I did not show up?

So, I got off at the next exit, made a left turn, and headed to the grocery store. When I got there, it was raining heavily. I chuckled, and said to God, "really! You are just testing me, to see if I would do it in the heavy rain!" He knew that I would. "Just don't let me have to walk too far," I said to God, jokingly.

I got to the door and motioned for a lady with her cart to go in ahead of me. About 30 steps in she stopped, and I stopped right beside her. I looked her in the eye and said, "I told God: don't let me have to walk too far to bless somebody." She gave me a smile and didn't say a word. Then I said, "I am here to bless somebody with a gift card, would you like to be blessed?" "Absolutely," she said with a smile. We talked briefly and I departed.

Giggling on the inside, all the way to my truck in the rain. I sat down in the truck, exhaled, and thought to myself, what just happened? I asked God, "why her?"

And He asked, "why not her? Do I need a reason to bless my children? She has been faithful, and I am blessing her through you." I got Goosebumps all over! Wow!

CHAPTER 43
An awesome day to be alive

After my second appointment was over, I headed into Giant for a few items. I'm always looking around to see who I can bless. Nobody caught my eye. I paid for my groceries and put them in my truck. I sat there but didn't feel that I could leave yet. A few minutes went by, then I saw someone walking towards the store at a very slow pace, with their foot in an air cast. I knew immediately I needed to find her in the store and talk to her. She grabbed a cart and headed inside. When I caught up with her, I could see that she had one item in the cart and had a distressed look on her face. I introduced myself and asked if there was anything I could do for her. With tears in her eyes, she asked, "like, what do you mean?" I replied, "I would like to give you a gift card towards your purchase today."

Now she's really crying. She finally got out a few words, "are you serious?" After taking a deep breath, she continued, "I'm really going through a rough patch. This means the world to me. Can I give you a hug?" We hugged, then talked for a while.

God knew her struggles. God was answering her prayers during a tough time.

Jeremiah 33:3a AMP
Call to me, and I will answer you.

The next one was sort of comical but hurt my feelings. I must be more aware of my Parkinson's tremor. When I get excited, I shake a lot. I approached her and asked if I could help. I could not finish my sentence before she brushed me off. Then I realized I probably look unapproachable with my tremor. Now I know to work on that before I walk up to someone.

OK, shaking it off, (no pun intended), looking for one more person to bless. I noticed a young lady with three children coming my way. I pulled out the card, took a breath and exhaled, "Good morning to this growing family. Can I ask you a question?" She replied, "sure." "May I bless you with a gift card towards your purchase today?" She smiled, and without hesitation, replied, "absolutely, with today's prices, that would be awesome. But why do you do this?" Open door! "My wife and I enjoy helping young families as they grow and work through the trials of life. God has blessed us, so we'd like to pass it on." With a big smile, she urged her children to say thank you, to the kind man. Her three-year-old daughter reached for the card, and said, "thank you."

No tears, no hugs, just pure joy to receive my gift! No matter how they respond, my soul is thrilled to give!

2 Corinthians 9:6-8 NIV

Remember this: Whoever sows sparingly will also reap sparingly, and whoever sows generously will also reap generously. Each of you should give what you have decided in your heart to give, not reluctantly or under compulsion, for God loves a cheerful giver.

It has been an incredible day. I still have a purpose. I feel like my cup is full and running over.

Thank you, Heavenly Father, for your guidance throughout my day.

CHAPTER 44

If you want to be used by God, just ask!

There are plenty of people who want their prayers answered. Do you want to be their answer? Can you believe that God will show you where they are?

I was not having a good morning. Parkinson's is rearing its ugly head. I was dropping things, spilling things. It's not pretty! Under my breath, I said, "I don't feel like ministering today. However, I already have plans to help people. God, can you use me despite how I feel?"

Suddenly, the nudge. "Now! Go." When this happens, I know to drop everything and drive, not knowing my destination until I am there. As I crossed the bridge to Columbia, I ordered a pizza for one of the homeless guys in the park. When I arrived with the pizza, he was not there. Maybe I didn't hear God and just wanted it to happen. But that wasn't "the nudge." As I drove up Chickies Hill, I turned into the park at the top of the hill. There were some cars parked there with nobody in them. I figured I just messed up again. Just then someone came walking across the lawn to the vehicle. I asked him if he would like a pizza from Domino's. He said he was hungry, and he gladly accepted it. As I was leaving, he gave me the thumbs up. I guess he liked it.

I must get ingredients to make zucchini bread for next Sunday's serve team dinner. I went to the Giant store in Mount Joy. I was almost in the store when I realized I forgot my prepaid Giant gift card! I had to go back to the truck for it. I like to carry a gift card in case I see an intended recipient. Going back to the truck, to me, was a timing issue to get me on track to be in the right place at the right time! I went into the store, got my items, and got into line at the cashier. Sometimes I'm a little too generous for my own good. Is that such a thing? I had one card, and almost gave it away, but I did not feel it was right. I got to my truck feeling a little disappointed that I did not give it away.

Sometimes a little too generous? Let me explain. Sometimes I just give. I think I would do better if I assessed the situation a little more. Sometimes I give to the first person that comes across my path, and the person that needs it is the second person that comes along. I've already given a card away and realized I gave it to the wrong person. Then I must go buy another card or live with the feeling.

I glanced sideways before backing out. I quickly put the truck into park and opened my window. I saw a lady with her child coming out of the Dollar Tree store. My heart started pounding. I was sure this was it. As she got beside my window, I asked, "can I ask you a quick question?" Stopping in her tracks, with a startled look on her face, she replied, "yes." "May I bless you with a Giant gift card today?" With tears and a smile, she replied, "yes, but are you sure?" "Absolutely sure, I was sitting here waiting for God to show me who I should give it to. Then you walked by my window."

Cupping her hands over her mouth and starting to cry, she replied, "you have no idea how bad I needed that today." She showed it to her daughter, both happy and crying. I was still sitting in my truck talking through my open window. She thanked me again and again. Then she wanted to give me a hug. I had to get out of my truck to oblige. As she hugged me, I assured her that God knows all about her needs. Then I said, "trust Him and He will meet them." Crying even harder now, she finally let go. You can tell when somebody's hug is sincere. Now I'm crying. They walked away towards the car, and the little girl turned around, as if to say, thanks again.

I'm back in my truck, looking for tissues to dry my eyes so I can drive home. Thinking to myself, should I have asked what more I can do? Should I have offered to do more, since they had such a need? I had to accept the fact that God knew I would walk away from that situation without asking those questions. I am at peace. I continued to weep all the way home.

Luke 11:9–10 ESV

And I tell you, ask, and it will be given to you; seek, and you will find; knock, and it will be opened to you. For everyone who asks receives, and the one who seeks finds, and to the one who knocks it will be opened.

Every time I step out of my house to go somewhere, I anticipate being used. I keep my eyes wide open, listening intently, wanting to seize the opportunity. Be an answer to somebody's prayer. You will be glad you did. Most people go to church on Sunday looking for God. I look for God every day. There are opportunities around every corner if you're looking.

CHAPTER 45
I love what I do

I was at a Giant store handing out gift cards again. Conversations are starting to get personal, so I am keeping it short and sweet for privacy reasons.

The first one was a single mother of three, struggling with finances but enjoying life with her children. I offered her a gift card. We talked a bit, and she was very thankful. You could tell she had a cheerful heart.

The second one was married with one child. She told me how hard it is to make ends meet. She graciously received a card, gave me a hug, and told me her name while shedding tears of joy.

I was prepared to give away four cards. I exited the store with two more in my hand. I used to be distraught over having extras, usually feeling like I didn't do or accomplish what I came for. But I have learned to be at peace. God is the author and finisher of my faith, and my story. When the time is right, these gift cards will find a home.

Sometimes I would go to a store and give a card to a person outside the store. If I didn't have a few in my pocket, I would have to go in and buy one quickly and hope I didn't miss an opportunity. I have had that happen several times.

Paul told Timothy in 2 Timothy 4:2 NIV, Preach the word; be prepared in season and out of season. That means you must always be ready, even if it is an inconvenient time for you. You must give yourself and your mind over to the lord.

CHAPTER 46
What? No raisins!

I need them for zucchini bread. God knew I would be out of raisins. I guess He's up to something. I headed to Giant for raisins.

I took a few gift cards into the store with me. I grabbed my items, paid the cashier, all the while looking around for opportunity. None! I headed to my truck. Right on my heels, was a young man with a baby in his cart. As I stopped, he went around me. I quickly said, "who do we have here?" referring to the baby. The young man stopped and proceeded to tell me. Then I asked, "how difficult is it to raise a family today, with prices being so high?" He replied, "there are always bills to pay! You pay one, and a few more pop up." He looked puzzled. I could see he wanted to know why I asked him that question. I proceeded, "then may I offer you a gift card for the next time you buy groceries?" "For real?" he questioned. "Why?" "Well, we raised our family, and we know the hardships that happen while your family is growing."

With such a sincere look on his face, he looked right into my eyes and said, "I am speechless! I don't know what to say." There it is . . . .that look! . . . priceless! "Blessings to you, brother. Have a great day."

If I ran out of raisins just for this moment, it was worth it!!! Yes, I enjoy blessing families, and it doesn't matter what age, gender, or race. God knows no boundaries. Divine appointments are special. Now, time to get home and make zucchini bread!

God literally commands the morning to set in order His loving kindness to be on full display!

Psalms 42:8 KJV

Yet the Lord will command his loving kindness in the daytime, and in the night his song shall be with me, and my prayer unto the God of my life.

CHAPTER 47
Don't wait for tomorrow!

I have four gift cards in my truck. We have no promise of tomorrow here on earth. So I want to give them away today.

I went to Giant to get what I needed. I grabbed my four gift cards and prayed over them, "Father, I know you can make a difference with these cards. Please help me find the right recipients. Thank You for allowing me to do this. I trust You to show me who needs them." I headed into the store, grabbed a cart, expedited getting the items on my list, and looked for potential recipients.

I saw a young mother looking at some items and putting them back. I approached her, and asked if she could use $50 off her grocery bill today. With a stunned look, and hesitation, she then said, "that would be great." As I handed her the gift card, she said, "you have no idea what this means to me." She was trying to attempt a smile through her tears. I told her my name, and said, "I've been where you are. I know that the struggles are real. I'm in a position where I can pay it forward." She then asked, "may I give you a hug?" We embraced as she wept.

Down the next aisle I met another woman, Casey, with her infant. I asked her if she would like a gift card toward her purchase. "I would prefer that you give it to somebody who needs it. We are doing OK. It is admirable what you are doing. It's so good to see somebody spreading kindness instead of hatred. I know people that are angry all the time. So, thanks, you've made my day just by asking." She started to walk away when I stopped her with another question. "How would you like to be the one giving away the card to someone else?" She thought about it for a few seconds, and said, "sure, I can do that, but do you trust me." "Absolutely, why would I not? You have been honest with me from the start." She thanked me and started to look around for somebody to bless.

As I turned around, I saw another person who I thought had witnessed what was going on. So I asked her if she could use a card. She said, "you really don't have to give me one just because I witnessed it happening." "But can you use it?" I asked her earnestly. "Yes, I can." "Then it's yours!" Her ear-to-ear grin said it all.

I paid for my groceries, and the cashier asked, "how many gift cards did you give away today?" I told her, "three." I know she will be listening for stories when those cards come through her line.

As I was departing, I saw Casey in a self-checkout line. She flagged me down. As I approached her, she said excitedly, "I gave it away! What a thrill to make somebody's day! To watch somebody, as their countenance changes." Then I said, "Casey, thank you for doing that!" She replied "thank you, for making my day. I won't forget that feeling."

Each one, reach one! Each one, teach one!

CHAPTER 48
Genuine prayer!

I had offered my "free turkey" certificate to someone. The certificate was linked to my account, so I had to be there to cash it in. I also had two gift cards with me to give away. So far, I haven't felt it. I paid for my groceries and got the free turkey. The person thanked me for the turkey and departed. I was at my truck loading my groceries when I felt the need to go back inside. Gift cards in hand, I started looking around.

I passed an elderly lady, who was driving an electric shopping cart. Something tugged at my heartstrings, but I kept walking. The further I got, the heavier I felt. I turned around and looked. She hadn't budged from where I passed her. I walked up to her, squatted down in front of her, and asked how she was doing. "I can't complain, God is good. I have aches and pains, but He sustains me." Wow, I thought, that sounds like me! I looked in her eyes and said, "may I bless you with a gift card today?" Looking away, she thought about it for a few seconds and looked right back at me with a grin. "Yes, you may," she replied softly. As she took the gift card, she noticed the Parkinson's tremor. "Give me your hand," she said, and then she started to pray. "Father, I thank you for this man who chose to be generous to me. Let Your hand be upon him." She continued with a very sweet prayer. I had shivers up my spine and throughout my body. I could sense God's presence. As she ended her prayer, I noticed people looking intently at me, squatting in front of her electric cart, holding her hand. Yes, a white man and a black woman blessing each other. I could imagine God saying let's take this show on the road. What a sense of humor for God to allow this to happen in the middle of a grocery store in plain sight for all to see. Such humility, on her part.

Now I'm walking around the store on cloud nine! I could hear an unhappy child in the distance. I could see he wanted a balloon. They were at different locations around the store. With a smile, I approached the mother with a gift card. "You have been kind to us several times, you don't have to again, unless you don't mind repeating." I replied, "I don't mind, it would be an honor giving to you again." She thanked me for the card, smiling as she walked away. Now, I'm almost in tears. Some people are once and done, others are repeats for God's glory.

CHAPTER 49
'Tis the season to give

Five days until Christmas! 'Tis the season to give! Shouldn't every day be the season to give?

It's the time of year that we enjoy family, food, and conversation. It is the time of year that we can give to others who are less fortunate.

At what length would you go to bless somebody? Our garbage trucks pick up around 4:30 AM every Wednesday. These guys are faithful in their job and provide a service that is unmatched. I woke up at 4 o'clock this morning, just to make sure that they would have a reward for their years' worth of effort. I let them pick out their own gift cards for restaurants. They were so appreciative! Cheerful "receivers" make my day and warm my heart.

Later today, Karen and I will be handing out care packages to the homeless consisting of cotton gloves, socks, hand warmers, snacks, fast food gift cards, and a bottle of water. Years ago, we stopped buying gifts for each other at Christmas and agreed to help the less fortunate.

We have a friend who has a dead battery. The battery is old. We are going to take her vehicle for a new battery. At 79 years old, she could use some assistance and guidance.

Who will God put in your path today? Keep your eyes wide open, and your heart listening. How will you bless somebody today? A kind word, a good deed?

Hebrews 13:16 ESV

Do not neglect to do good and to share what you have, for such sacrifices are pleasing to God.

CHAPTER 50
Back on track, Timing is key

I wanted to leave home at 8:30 am. I had a full schedule planned. Do you want to make God laugh? Tell Him your plans for today!

Around 9:00 am I was pulling out of the driveway. I was headed one way, when I thought I needed to turn and go in a different direction. Now heading to the Mount Joy Food Bank, I dropped off items that were donated from the Mount Joy campus. As I left the building, I knew this wasn't my appointment, but it put me in the correct timing. As I turned the corner with my truck, I saw a postal worker delivering mail. I gave her some McDonald's cards over a month ago. I instructed her to give one away, and she could have the other. I pulled beside her, called her by name, then gave her a few more cards. When she asked why I blessed her, that opened the door for witnessing. All I will say is the conversation was good. I knew there was a reason for coming in this direction.

I headed towards Manheim. There is a family that likes my homemade chili. I haven't seen them in a while, but

I felt like it was time to drop some off. I put it on the porch, 32° outside. I called the husband and told him where it was. He said that was awesome, his wife was sick and still in bed. Now they could have supper without her having to cook something. I did not know she was sick, I was just following God's lead. I sent her a text with a prayer for her healing. I found out later that she got up shortly after that, ate some of the chili, and felt great the rest of the day.

We are all called to minister to people. Here am I, Lord, send me. The rest of my day fell into place better than I could have planned it. I am amazed at the intricacy of God's timing.

Psalm 37:23-24 NKJV
The steps of a good man are ordered by the Lord, And He delights in his way. Though he falls, he shall not be utterly cast down; for the Lord upholds him with his hand.

CHAPTER 51
Kingdom purposes

Great timing; called to have church in the grocery store. Two days ago I had a molar extracted to try to relieve the pain from trigeminal neuralgia. I was having a rough time at Parkinson's therapy this morning, so they decided to release me early. Little did I know that this was a ministry timing thing.

I went to Giant to get ingredients so I could make zucchini bread tomorrow. I had three gift cards in my pocket to give away. After I filled my cart, I noticed a mother with four kids. I approached her and asked if I could bless them with a gift card. She immediately started to cry and asked, "are you sure?" I assured her that I wanted to. "Why?" she asked. "Because I know what it's like to raise a growing family." These are the moments that thrill my heart. Pure joy flows as I walk away.

The next one has three children. I approached and offered a gift card to help with her purchase. She proceeded to tell me the story of how they needed it. I fully understand what that's like.

I was headed to the cash register when I felt a nudge to go down an aisle that I had already been down. I saw a young man with his toddler. They were looking at juices but walked away without one. That was a clue that they might not be able to afford it. I stopped him and asked if I could bless him with a gift card. He started to weep. He said, "you have no idea how we need this." He shook my hand, and he said, "my wife is right behind you." As I turned around, he said, "honey, this man just blessed us with a card for our purchase today." She started to cry. "We had a terrible week financially. Both our cars went into the shop this week. Your timing is amazing!" Without hesitation, I had decided I could do more. I told them I would give them $500 towards the car repairs. You want to talk about genuine emotion. We were having church, right there in the grocery store.

Had I left my therapy any time later, I would have missed these opportunities. While God is not limited to time, He uses time for His glory. He redeems the time for kingdom purposes.

I've been asking God for grace. For Him to walk with me while I go through this season in my life: Parkinson's with a tremor, therapy to regain dexterity in my left hand, dealing with trigeminal neuralgia and its excruciating jaw pain, Tinnitus so loud hearing aids can't help, and at times, having vertigo related to Ménière's Disease. I have reached a pinnacle where I can see why people contemplate taking their life. Pain so great, some nights I desire to fall asleep and wake up in eternity. But it's not my choice. I wake up each day, wondering how

God will use me. Through the pain, through the suffering, He will make a way. I can't imagine the pain leading up to the cross. I am weak, yet He is strong.

John 16:33 NIV
I have told you these things, so that in me you may have peace. In this world you will have trouble. But take heart! I have overcome the world.

Isaiah 43:2 NLT
When you go through deep waters, I will be with you. When you go through rivers of difficulty, you will not drown. When you walk through the fire of oppression, you will not be burned up; the flames will not consume you.

CHAPTER 52
No gift cards, no hype

I said to God, "I will go to the grocery store and do what you've called me to do, but it would be nice if I could see that it is not always about money." I felt God saying in response, "but you're one person I can trust with money." "OK God, have it your way."

It was another rough morning with Parkinson's. I did not want to drive until I felt it was safe. Around 10:30 am, I felt I was OK to drive. I gave out more gift cards today than I had all last week. So much for the prayer of not costing me anything! If they're in my pocket, I give them away. Maybe I won't buy so many at one time (yeah, right, like that will happen).

God chose later that day as the day to answer the prayer of not costing any money. I needed distilled water for our humidifiers. The only store that has that locally is SKH. My goal was to buy water last Friday or Saturday. It did not happen. What happened today says it all. I put three cases of water in my cart. I wanted to find organic baked beans. I have no idea why I was craving baked beans today. Wait for it! There was a cart sitting right in front of the baked beans. I patiently waited for the person to move it. As she apologized, I said, "no problem, I think you are right where you're supposed to be." With that dazed look, as to why I made such a statement, I continued the conversation. "God brought me here, to be here for you." Sounds a little bold. Sometimes even I wonder, but I am here for a purpose. "I told her that I go through grocery stores looking for people who are asking God for answers. Now she is really interested. We talked for about 20 minutes. She is new to the area. She is looking for a church, but one that does not have loud rock music. She was at a local church and did not like the noise. She said she prefers hymns like she grew up with. I suggested a few churches that have that atmosphere. She watches services online. I commend her for that. Now she is really intrigued with what I do. At one point, almost in tears, she touched my elbow and said, "I really needed to hear this. You are so bold at what you do. I wish I had that tenacity." I assured her she could start anywhere, anytime. Then I asked her how I could pray for her today. She was very specific, and then started asking more questions about me. I replied, "I'm just the hands and feet of Jesus." She was honored and challenged to have met me. We exchanged names so I could pray for her.

No gift cards, no hype, just one on one conversation. It did not cost me a penny, just as I prayed earlier. God may not answer when we want, but rather, when we need it.

Joshua 1:9 NIV

Have I not commanded you? Be strong and courageous. Do not be afraid; do not be discouraged, for the Lord your God will be with you wherever you go.

CHAPTER 53
Song: Truth Be Told by Matthew West

This song by Matthew West totally embodies a sermon I heard on Sunday. "I'm fine, yes I'm fine; but I'm not, I'm broken."

I watch the confusion on people's faces when they see me with Parkinson's. My tremor is uncontrollable. When I am asked how I am doing, I just say I'm fine, because it seems like nobody has "time" for the real answer. I put on a good face and show them I am a Christian living above the circumstances. Then I am hard on myself for not responding honestly. There are days that take everything I have to get through them. I am in a "season," and I am aware of it. Wherever I am, The Great "I AM" is with me!

To God be the glory for whatever he chooses to take me through. Truth be told, I have not fallen into despair; I have fallen into Grace.

We are all going through stuff! We must pick ourselves up every time we fall, but we do not have to lie about falling. Through the falling we continue to grow. The last two years dealing with Parkinson's and vertigo have been the hardest of my life. But it was very instrumental in becoming who I am now.

Truth Be Told

Lie number one: You're supposed to have it all together
And when they ask how you're doin', just smile and tell them, "Never better"
Lie number two: Everybody's life is perfect except yours
So keep your messes and your wounds and your secrets safe with you behind closed doors

But truth be told
The truth is rarely told, no...

I say, "I'm fine, yeah, I'm fine, oh, I'm fine, hey, I'm fine"
But I'm not, I'm broken
And when it's out of control I say it's under control
But it's not and You know it
I don't know why it's so hard to admit it
When bein' honest is the only way to fix it
There's no failure, no fall
There's no sin You don't already know
So let the truth be told

There's a sign on the door, says, "Come as you are" but I doubt it

'Cause if we lived like that was true, every Sunday
mornin' pew would be crowded
But didn't You say church should look more like a
hospital?
A safe place for the sick, the sinner and the scarred,
and the prodigals, like me

But truth be told, the truth is rarely told
Oh, am I the only one who says...

"I'm fine, yeah, I'm fine, oh, I'm fine, hey, I'm fine"
But I'm not, I'm broken
And when it's out of control I say it's under control
But it's not and You know it
I don't know why it's so hard to admit it
When bein' honest is the only way to fix it
There's no failure, no fall
There's no sin You don't already know
So let the truth be told

Can I really stand here unashamed
Knowin' that Your love for me won't change?
Oh God, if that's really true
Then let the truth be told

I say, "I'm fine, yeah, I'm fine, oh, I'm fine, hey, I'm
fine"
But I'm not, I'm broken
And when it's out of control I say it's under control
But it's not and You know it

I don't know why it's so hard to admit it
When bein' honest is the only way to fix it
There's no failure, no fall
There's no sin You don't already know
Yeah, I know
There's no failure, no fall
There's no sin You don't already know
So let the truth be told

CHAPTER 54
The downside of illness

When I get ill, I tend to be an island unto myself. I do not let people in. I need people to surround me with prayer, so that they can rejoice when their faith has been exercised and prayers have been answered. Forgive me for my ignorance.

I am tired. It is the kind of tiredness that you can't sleep off. What is hard is knowing how it affects me, one single person. What is harder is knowing how it affects other people around me.

I am having a few bad days. Back to work for my wife. She does not want to leave my side, but she must. We sat on the sofa and held each other this morning. I cannot imagine what she feels. She sees my struggles but cannot help. We cry to God, but I am not healed. As she left for work, I dozed off.

I continue to pray for God to use me. Around 8:00 AM, I suddenly awakened. "Now, get ready to go." God knows how long it will take me to get ready. I am confident of His timing. About 40 minutes later, I was heading out the door. Gift cards in hand, I went to the Giant grocery store. My head felt clear for a brief time to minister. I grabbed four items that I needed from the store. Then I looked for somebody to bless.

The first mother with her child turned me down. "You offered to me many times, but I still have to say no. Please find someone who can use it. But it is sweet, what you do."

Being a little bit frustrated, I asked God to bring someone to me. Within seconds, literally, a mother with two children came through the door. She saw me, then looked the other way, and tried to pass by me. "Excuse me, ma'am, may I ask you a question?" Then she smiled and said yes. "How would you like to start your new year with an extra $50 towards your groceries today?" She gracefully accepted. The kids were saying thank you, so I asked them where they would like to eat lunch today. They said McDonald's! I pulled out some McDonald's gift cards and handed them to their mother. It is even more special when the kids get involved and they are thankful.

A few aisles down there was another family, thankful for help with their groceries. Her face lit up with a big smile and tears. My heart goes out to those who struggle.

I am in my truck, ready to leave, but hesitated. Something is not finished. Thirty seconds later a car rolled through, circled around, and parked near me. "Give them some gift cards" is what I heard. I got out of my truck and approached them. As he opened his window, I recognized him from a few weeks ago. I gave them cards at that time. I offered him some more, and he said, "no, you already did enough." I did not want to be disrespectful, but I knew what God told me to do. So, I offered him the cards in a different way. "If you know somebody who can use them, please give it to them. I am giving you seed so that you can plant and reap the harvest." "I can do that," he said. We talked for a few minutes, and then I went on my way.

When my life is over, let it not be said that I was selfish. But rather, "Whatever is mine is yours. If you need it, it is yours! God will give me more."

I am sitting here, listening to worship songs, and crying my eyes out! I am realizing how great God has been to me, thankful for my wife, Karen, that He gave me, now realizing how fragile life really is.

CHAPTER 55
No more TV

I started to feel better around 2 PM. Today we ended our TV cable subscription. It jumped $120 from the initial promotional program, and we do not want to pay $280 a month to have cable and Internet. No more TV! I cannot justify $280 a month when people are homeless and hungry. I sat on my Lazy Boy and took a nap. I needed the rest. (Please understand I do not think my conviction about TV applies to everyone. Please allow God to guide you. This is my story; this is my journey.)

I went to the Mount Joy Giant today to buy more gift cards to hand out. I paid for my groceries and the gift cards. I looked around and it did not seem like any opportunities at this time. I left the building and put things in my truck. Then I saw a mother and child walk into the store. Opportunity knocks! I just can't resist going back in and making someone smile.

When they came to a stop inside the store, I asked if I could bless them with a gift card towards their purchase. I was sad when they turned me down. We did have a conversation that lifted my spirit. She thanked me for what I was doing, and I thanked her for her honesty.

As I turned to walk away, I knew the next one was right. Jokingly I asked, "is it expensive to raise kids nowadays?" We laughed together at such a question. I offered her a $50 gift card, and there it is! That look is priceless! With tears now flowing, she asked if she could give me a hug. Absolutely! I know now that this is why I came back into the store. I love my calling!

As I continue to walk in my current situation, Parkinson's, and neurological issues, I must learn to rest in Him. Strength comes from climbing the mountain, not having it removed. Forgive me, Father; Your kingdom come; Your will be done. Continue Your work in me.

CHAPTER 56
Up to some good!

Almost noon time, I was starting to feel that call. As I pulled into a parking space, I noticed a young mother with two children loading their car with groceries. All my gift cards in hand, I approached the car. I read the bumper sticker that said something about her having a bad attitude because of her kids. Judgment set in, I started to walk away with such a conviction in my spirit. God said, "who do you think you are? Did I not tell you to bless her?" Immediately I melted in repentance. I turned around, and the car was still there. I tapped on the window and got that stare. Like, what do you want? The window opened, and so did my opportunity. "Where would you guys like to eat lunch today?"

Caught off guard, she hesitated and said, "we like Burger King." I have a few of those! After I handed gift cards to her, she asked why? I told her that we like to bless families that are growing. She started to cry, and then asked if she could give me a hug. Before I could say yes, she was out of the car, with her arms wrapped around my neck. After she told me some of her story, I offered her a $50 card for her next grocery purchase. Now the tears are really flowing, followed by another hug. As I watched, from inside the store, I could see it took a while to dry the tears to be able to drive. How impressive is our God!

Wow, what a start. I cannot wait to see who is next. As I turned around, there was a mother. Her toddler was trying desperately to get bananas from mom. She kept saying no, it was not in the budget. I asked her if I could bless her with a $50 card towards her purchase. She hesitantly received the card and thanked me. She wanted to know more of my story. We talked for a while. She had four other children at home. Now I realized her little boy was hungry. I asked her where he likes to eat. She said Wendy's. I gave her a gift card to Wendy's as she was helping the little boy put bananas in the cart. I grabbed a few bananas. She thanked me again as I was walking away. As I turned to say you're welcome, the tears were flowing. She could not contain it anymore. She was grateful. Under my breath I am whispering, "please God, send her ministering angels." I have no idea what triggered it. But it felt good.

I paid for my items and put them in my truck. I grabbed some more gift cards, to head back in. I stopped just outside the door and noticed a woman with a child, and another woman in the distance with her child. It felt like a mistake to get one without the other, they almost collided. In reaction, my body turned away. I ended up facing the one that needed ministered to. (I did not know it at that time, but I know it was a God thing). I asked if

I could bless her with a gift card. She accepted with a smile. Her little girl said thank you without any prompting, then came mom's question. "Do you take prayer requests?" "Absolutely!" I replied. She told me the story about the doctors trying to help her daughter, Olivia, get more sleep. She sleeps about two hours a night. Doctors want to put her on steroids and continue the shots to "experiment" with the situation. I told her that we will be praying and invited her to church. They moved here from Harrisburg and were looking for a local church. That led to a conversation with an invite to Victory Church, Mount Joy, PA.

Please pray for Olivia that she will sleep peacefully from this day on. Pray for the family that they will continue to serve God and find a church home.

I thank God for His divine appointments. I could not time it any better. What a formidable God!

As I'm sitting in my house, I am presented with two more opportunities. Today we got an Amazon and UPS delivery. I gave them both restaurant gift cards. I'm watching grown men, nearly in tears, thankful for the gift. When they leave my place, they know they are appreciated.

I remember the time when my garbage guy responded in this way: "I never knew my services were appreciated. Thank you for telling me, and for the gift card. It means a lot."

Every day there is an opportunity. Eyes wide open, everybody looking around: who needs your encouragement?

CHAPTER 57
The power of generosity revisited

Two years ago, I was writing in my journal about the power of generosity. When you start to minister to somebody, are you ready for more? Are you all in? Or do you just want convenience? We say, "save them Father God," and then we turn them over to the pastor or special groups as we walk away. Do we just want to half -help, but nothing more? Nothing more because we don't have the time, or we are not really invested. Are we being partially generous, or do we give until it hurts? What decisions have you made that are creating your legacy?

Recently, I saw that God is testing me in generosity. I told a friend of mine who had been recently incarcerated that I would help him get back on his feet financially. His vehicles were sitting for three years. I had an 8 o'clock appointment to take him for a battery to put in his truck. I committed to helping him get two trucks back on the road so he could get back to work. I offered to loan him $800 cash to get started. This would help him get his driver's license, insurance, and extra cash until he got his first paycheck. He's self-employed as a contractor.

Vehicles are important to what he does for people. I'm excited to see how God will work this out. After we got the battery and installed it, the truck fired up on the first try.

Then we grabbed all the paperwork for both trucks and headed to AAA to renew the registrations and to get insurance on them. I prayed that God would give us qualified people to help us. I also prayed we would get out of there quickly. Apparently, you can't have your cake and eat it too! 3 1/2 hours later, the task was over. However, with that said, we did have very qualified people who made it very easy for us, but it took time. We got what we came for. Now the trucks could be inspected, which should be the final hurdle before he can get back to work.

I thought that was the end of it. I figured I could do another $1,200 and that would be it, but things had rusted and corroded during his three-year stint in prison; my heart balked! I have done enough. Now the total to date was $3,800! Almost five times my original intent! I had an attitude. God intervened, "take a deep breath and stick to your commitment. There are souls at stake. Where will they spend eternity?" God reminded me that we are the hands and feet of Jesus and sometimes the finances! How far are you willing to go so that one person would be saved? I can rest peacefully, knowing that I did my part. How my friend responds to God is on him.

Giving: I do not give to get. I give so that I can give some more. Setting goals for giving is a good start.

Proverbs 11:25 TPT

Those who live to bless others will have blessings heaped upon them, and the one who pours out his life to pour out blessings will be saturated with favor.

CHAPTER 58
Off to the market, wanting to minister!

I went to SKH in Mount Joy, bought some gift cards, then I started walking through the store. I noticed some organic products that I could use in making chili. So, I grabbed a cart, grabbed a few items, and headed to the register. I was next in line when I recognized the cashier. I met her outside Dollar Tree a few weeks ago. We must have talked for 30 minutes about faith, church, and family. I invited her to church since she was new to the area. She did show up the following week while we were visiting family elsewhere. She proceeded to tell me that she loved it. She talked with the pastor about his son's disability because her grandson has a similar disability. She told me she would be back. We talked some more, until other people got in line. We said goodbye. This is another story that will continue to unfold. Blessing other people opens new doors.

Next, I went to Dollar Tree hoping to pick up a few items for the food bank in Elizabethtown which had given me specifics. However, the store did not have what they wanted. The Giant store is next door. I went in to see if I could find some of the products.

Gift cards are in my pocket! As I entered, an elderly lady was exiting. She turned and walked back in without her cart and grabbed a banana that is free for small children. She did not have many groceries, so I offered her a gift card towards her next purchase. She immediately had her arms around my neck. Hugging me and thanking me for my kindness. As she walked away, I heard her say, "I can't believe he did that for me."

As I grabbed my favorite granola and turned the corner, I came across another couple that I helped several weeks ago. At that time, I remember offering them cards, but they refused to take them because I had helped them previously. When they refused, I offered them again, suggesting that they find someone who needed them. I was giving seed for them to plant! Today, as I met them, they have an incredible story to tell. Now they understand how I feel when I give. Remember, I only went into the store because the other store did not have what I wanted! That is a God thing!! It does not end there.

I paid for my groceries and put them in my truck. Then I grabbed some restaurant cards to hand out. As I turned around, I saw a mother and child heading to their car while the dad stayed behind to pay for the groceries. The child was in tears. This was the same family that I just talked to inside. I headed towards the entrance, knowing that God's timing is awesome. I had wanted to give them more Chick-fil-A cards. The parents told the daughter last time when I gave them cards to give away that she had to give them all away without eating there. She was not happy about that. I want to look at things through a child's eyes. Now I am standing there, wondering what I am to do. Just like that, the wife drove up and parked right beside me. It was now raining, and she was going to pick up her husband when he came out with the groceries. She opened the window to talk. I asked the daughter if she would like to have a Chick-fil-A card. Through her tears, she said yes. Then I asked, if I give you three cards, will you give one away and keep two for yourself? She said yes again. Now the child is happy. While she is learning to give cards away, I think she needs to be rewarded. She needs to know that God is good, and He will bless you when you give.

Proverbs 22:6 NKJV
Train up a child in the way that they should go, and when they are old they will not depart from it.

CHAPTER 59
A Lesson in humility! Part 1

After my tooth extraction, I started developing a bone spur that was coming through the gum line. Today it was sharp and cut my tongue. I got an appointment and arrived with two minutes to spare. The assistant took me back right away, prepared me, then left the room. 20 minutes... 30 minutes... 40 minutes. At the 45-minute mark, I started to take offense at being abandoned. I opened the door and asked if they had forgotten about me. They assured me that they did not, but I could tell they did! About 10 minutes later, the dental surgeon came in, took care of the problem, gave me care instructions, then left the room. Within seconds of his departure, the assistant grabbed my wrist to get my attention. "I wanted you to know, this was not the doctor's fault, but mine. I take full responsibility. It was my fault that you have been here so long, not his. I am so sorry!!" Then the Holy Spirit prompted me, "you need to verbally accept her apology." With Parkinson's, I don't always get the words out the way I want to, but I blurted out, "accepted." Then she let go on my wrist, threw her arms around me, and said, "Thank you!" She cried happy tears. She followed me to the exit and thanked me again as we said goodbye. My forgiveness meant something to her!

I sat in my truck, feeling like I just got schooled in humility! I commend her for owning her mistake. I am thankful that the Holy Spirit prompted me because forgiveness is powerful. Her humble heart melted mine. The look on her face after she hugged me was priceless. What a lesson!

We have so many opportunities that test our Christianity. Do we respond like Christ? Do others see Christ in you? Every day presents new opportunities. Rise to the occasion with a compassionate heart!

Colossians 3:12-13 NLT

Since God chose you to be the holy people he loves, you must clothe yourselves with tenderhearted mercy, kindness, humility, gentleness, and patience. Make allowance for each other's faults and forgive anyone who offends you. Remember, the Lord forgave you so you must forgive others.

A lesson in humility! Part 2

How many times do we start the process of forgiveness, but we don't finish it? My previous lesson in humility taught me that we need to finish the forgiveness which was asked of us. If we don't say, "apology accepted," then do we really forgive them? Do we need to say it for their clarity? Do they feel forgiven when they walk away? Let's finish the process!

A lesson in humility! Part 3

The story continues: Another bone spur is coming through the gum line. I was not happy! Why is this happening? Who am I to argue with God? You will soon see why I say this.

I arrived at the oral surgery center. One of the dental associates was shoveling the sidewalk. Whoever did the original snow removal did not do the sidewalk correctly. She was not happy with their shoddy work. I told her that I am a fan of working hard. So, I gave her a gift card to Olive Garden. She refused it at first. But she does like to eat there. I finally convinced her to take it.

I signed in and waited my turn. I was called to come in and to my surprise, it was the assistant who owned up to her mistake the last time I was in. She was so happy to see me that she gave me a big hug. After we got through the formalities of why I was there, I pulled out some gift cards for her to choose from. She wanted to know why. I told her that I appreciated her honesty, that she owned the situation, and she had challenged me to be a better person. "You're going to make me cry," she said. I told her that I was really challenged by her actions of integrity. I told her that I am writing a book called *Parkinson's: With Purpose*. I explained some of the things that I do, since I no longer go fishing. I used to be an angler of fish, now I am a fisherman of souls, trying to do good and bless people wherever I go.

Every day you are in contact with people. Why not have purpose with them? Were you put in their path for a reason? I say it repeatedly: eyes wide open, ears listening, who is your mission today?

Some people are a one-time thing. Some people are for a season. Few are for a lifetime. Learn to discern. Then you will not be so unhappy when someone leaves your life. Take what you have learned and build on it. You were meant to do remarkable things, even if it is just trivial things. Be faithful in what you are called to do. Big or small, it's all part of God's plan. We can't all be Billy Graham, Martin Luther King, or Mother Teresa. But we can be who God intended us to be!

CHAPTER 60
A Night of Bradycardia!

Parkinson's disease is a neurological condition. Other issues that are neurological can accompany Parkinson's. Bradycardia is when heart rates drop below 50 BPM. Last night I had over 20 episodes ranging from 36 to 42 BPM. I exercised for 60 minutes this morning only to get my heart rate up to 52 BPM. I have nothing on my schedule today, wondering, "God, how can you use me when I feel like this?"

At 11:00 AM I felt the nudge to "go now." Ok God, give me strength. I was heading towards the supermarket and decided to go to the Mount Joy Food Bank instead. I like to be updated on what they need. From there I went to Giant. In my pocket, I had Giant gift cards of different amounts.

My first encounter turned me down. "Please find somebody who can use it. We are doing OK." So, I decided to get the groceries I came for, and let things just happen. Usually, I bump into somebody who can use it. It did not take long. I noticed a cart full of kids and groceries coming towards me. I bided my time. This looked like it could be a double opportunity for me: grocery cards and lunch cards. "Excuse me, do you have time to talk?" It is a loaded question when you have four kids who can't stand still. To my amazement the kids were intrigued at my question and were all being very attentive.

Before I could ask the question about the gift card, she stopped me and said, "you have done this before, you've been a blessing, but you can find someone else to bless? I do not want to double dip and get another card." I am thinking; four kids, lots of groceries, how can you not use it? I pulled a handful of cards out of my pocket, and said, "if you can use it, I would like to bless you." She thanked me and told me that she homeschooled the kids and they were on lunch break right now. Ah ha! That opened the door for the second question. "What are you doing for lunch?"

"When I get home with the groceries, I will make lunch while they are studying." I offered her some restaurant cards so that she could have a break from cooking. She declined. "We do not eat out. That's a treat we just cannot afford." "Well, I am offering 'to afford it' for you. You're a mother and a teacher. You deserve a break today." It sounded like a McDonald's commercial to me. Now, remember, the kids were paying close attention to things I was saying. As soon as I asked mom where they would like to eat, three shouted, "McDonald's," one shouted "Domino's Pizza." I could see her getting emotional when I handed her several McDonald's cards and one Domino's Pizza card. I wish you could have heard the peanut gallery cheering and clapping. The kids were all smiling about going out to eat. I think, in secret, mom was glad too!

I really like blessing people. It does not have to be divine. I just like to do it. Every now and then I can tell when something is my divine appointment. There is more spiritual depth to it. The timing from one encounter leads to the timing of another encounter.

My eyes were drawn to a young lady at the salad bar. Before she had a chance to start, I asked her if I could buy her lunch. "OK, I think? But why?" I replied, "I just want to make your day and do something nice for you." She said, "Well, thank you, that's awesome."

I paid for my items but felt a strong tug: do not leave! I moved to a spot where I could observe every register. I saw a young lady in a hurry, checking out by herself. Oh yeah, this is it! This is the right timing! "Excuse me, can I offer you a gift card towards your purchase?" "That would be incredible! My son had surgery today and I am trying to do this quickly and get home." "May I ask his name, so I can pray for him?" "Yes, let me show you a picture of him. He has a rare disease that causes water to build up in his belly. Then he gets hernias that must be operated on." Now we are both in tears. I feel her pain! Through the tears I assured her one more time that we would be praying for him. She thanked me, and I went on my way. I looked back to see her wiping her eyes and bagging groceries.

This is what I live for!

Psalm 34:19 TPT
Even when bad things happen to the good and godly ones, the Lord will save them and not let them be defeated by what they face.

CHAPTER 61
Bring them to me

Time to give away gift cards! I still have a few gift cards in my pocket. If I wait till tomorrow, I could miss a blessing. If I wait till tomorrow, it could be too late. What good is a card that is not used? Let's do this!

I parked at the grocery store, made my way inside, looked around, and thought, where do I start? It is a Friday night crowd. I froze in my tracks. "Father, bring them to me."

Just then, a man of great stature walked in with his two kids. I blurted out, "may I bless you with a gift card towards your purchase today?" Without hesitation, "yes you may!" He told me his name, thanked me, and we both walked away with a big smile.

As I was turning around, I just missed a mother with her two kids. I caught up to her as she was loading her cart and placed a gift card on her groceries while she was watching me. Through her tears, in a low volume, she said, "thank you!"

Now, as I am walking past the registers, I see another opportunity and put a gift card on top of the groceries. She was speechless. I smiled and walked away.

As I was exiting the store, a young mother with her two children was trying to find the firetruck cart. The young man was crying because someone else was using it. I offered them a McDonald's card. He stopped crying and said, "thank you."

I have seen so many well-behaved, well-mannered children over the last few months. I give credit to the mothers of this generation. I also gave her a Giant gift card. Oh, the joy of giving!

That night, I got a text message from a friend at church. I share this part of the story only to show that people are grateful. My friend's text said, "on the Mount Joy page on FB they are talking about an older gentleman giving out gift cards at Giant. "Thank you to the older gentleman who walked up to me and my kids while grocery shopping at Giant and placed a gift card in my cart. You give me hope in humanity!"

I then prayed, Father, I give You the glory. You get all the credit. Without You, I can do nothing. You give me grace to do these things in your name. You show me great mercy as I battle through Parkinson's Disease. You give me strength when I am weak. You guide my footsteps when it is hard to walk. You have blessed me abundantly. Amen

CHAPTER 62
Swing and a miss!

I am generally good at knowing who to ask. My truck would be ready for me at the collision center. I could pick it up and return the rental. My time to get it was 10:30 AM. It was 9:15 am

AM now, just enough time to give away gift cards at Giant. I had six cards in my pocket. Divine appointments or not, I am giving these away.

I was talking to someone while waiting in line at the information center. He was saying that he buys walkers and canes at yard sales and donates them to charity. I am intrigued by how many ways there are to give. I commended him on his efforts.

As he started to talk to the cashier, I turned around to give away cards, almost running into a mother and her two children. "Would you like to have a gift card towards your purchase today?" "No, we're good!" she said with an attitude. Without hesitation she walked away.

Not everybody is willing to take money from a stranger with a hand tremor (Parkinson's). Swing and a miss! OK, moving on. There are a lot of families here this morning, probably because there is snow in the forecast.

The next family was a mother with three children. I offered to bless her with a gift card. Quickly snatching the card from my hand and thinking it was a prank, she saw the amount on the card. Followed by great laughter, she said, "are you serious? This is incredible!" She proceeded to tell me her name, and the kids' names. Getting the card could not have happened at a better time. She was so excited, telling me that she is currently pregnant! I asked her children where they would like to eat lunch. Without hesitation, the three of them blurted out McDonald's. I pulled out my stash of cards and gave them a few for McDonald's. The kids started jumping up and down, screaming and laughing.

One Giant card down, five more to go. The next person was trying to get eggs out of the refrigerator section. When I interrupted, she thought I was talking to someone else. Then she noticed me standing there with the card in my hand. "Oh, you're talking to me?" Looking at the card and saying, "sure, I'll take that," as she put the third carton of eggs in the cart. Nothing more said, I moved on.

The next one was coming right at me with no food in the cart. She was a young mother with three children. I asked, "are you just getting started?" It was obvious, so why did I ask? She could not get around me, so she stopped. "I am handing out gift cards today, could you use one?" I could see her processing the offer in her mind, and she finally said, "sure." The look on her face, when she saw the amount on the card, priceless!

This next event was witnessed by a cashier, who talked to me about it days later. As I turned the corner, I saw two boys in the cart, but no parents. Their mother was crouched down, looking for something on the bottom shelf. "Do you need any help?" I offered. She got up and looked at me strangely. Before she could say anything, I put a gift card in her hand. "Why, thank you!" Then she saw the amount on the card and gasped! Then came the hug! That's when I get all choked up.

Walking past the cash registers, I noticed a young mother with two children patiently waiting for her turn to check out. "This is for you," I said, handing her the card. "I don't know what to say but thank you." I said, "you're welcome."

I strolled the aisles for about ten more minutes, wanting to give away the final card. It just was not happening. Before I exited, I talked to a cashier who knew me and my mission. By now, the young mother with her two kids had left the store. The cashier said, "you really made her day." She had asked the cashier, "why did he pick me?" I told her you just randomly pick people and bless them. We laughed and talked for a while.

Now I'm in the truck, emptying my pocket, realizing I still have one more card. I see a mother with two kids coming towards me. I opened the window, handed her the card and she thanked me as I pulled away. Then I heard her shriek when she saw the amount.

To God, be the glory, great things He has done. Another day in the life of Parkinson's. God is using me in ways that I have never expected.

CHAPTER 63
Loading for opportunities!

Since I am low on gift cards, I need to restock. I miss opportunities when I am not prepared. When I arrived at the Giant parking lot, I noticed a possibility. I had two McDonald's cards left, so I put them in my pocket and headed towards a mom who was putting her infant in the car along with her other kids. I asked, "are you guys getting hungry yet?" "Yes, she replied, we are just trying to figure out where we're going." "Do you eat at McDonald's?" "Oh, my kids love it there!" "So be it! I would like to buy you lunch." I handed her two McDonald's cards, and the kids were jumping and screaming thank you.

That was the end of my supply, so I went into Giant to buy some more. I got an assortment of Burger King, Wendy's, McDonald's, Domino's Pizza, and Giant cards. Total today $600. That should last a while. One year ago, we could only afford $100 a month. I believe through tithing and giving that God has given the increase. We had planned to give more this year. It seemed that the more we gave, the more our income increased. There are months when I don't spend anything extra on Parkinson's. Those months I can give more. In the months that I need testing or need to go to the emergency room, money goes towards Parkinson's issues. But by the grace of God, He has given us an increase.

Luke 6:38 CEB

Give, and it will be given to you. A good portion— packed down, firmly shaken, and overflowing—will fall into your lap. The portion you give will determine the portion you receive in return.

After I finished the purchase, the cashier started to tell me about what she was seeing. Two days ago, a lady came in from the parking lot to make sure the card that I gave her was real. She said, "it happened so fast. He came up to me and said this is his last card, and he's giving it to me."

The cashier said, "I assured her that the card was good, and that this is what he does." Then the cashier proceeded to tell me, "It was incredible to see you in action the other day. You were making your rounds and made your way back through the store to where I was. I saw firsthand how you interact with people. That lady with her children was crying when you walked away. It must be a great feeling for you." "Yes, it was. I gave away six Giant cards that day. Every one of them was grateful for the help."

As I was walking out the door, I noticed someone who looked familiar. I offered her a gift card. She looked at me sadly. "I keep turning you down when you ask. I feel like I am taking away from somebody who really needs it." "But can you use it?" I asked. As I put the card in her hand, I said, "please take it, this time." Her smile was awesome! Some people need a nudge to receive a blessing.

Mathew 6:1 NLT
Watch out! Don't do your good deeds publicly, to be admired by others, for you will lose the reward from your Father in heaven.

I walk a fine line when it comes to this scripture. I'm in the public, blessing people. I don't do it to be admired, but for the satisfaction of helping somebody. I cannot help it if other people see what I'm doing. How they interpret it is up to them. I find that most of the cashiers get excited when they see me walk in. They know something good is going to happen. And at times they get to be part of that. Recipients will often share their stories with the cashiers. They tell me stories that I would never have known otherwise.

Around 30 years ago, I was the one who needed help financially. I had two years of struggles due to a health condition. At that time, I could not afford groceries, so now I can feel their pain. I was homeless another time after a painful divorce, so now I give back to that community, too.

Sometimes I feel that any day now I could go home to be with God. I know I can't take the finances with me. I choose to help others before I exit this earth. I have to realize that I was created for heaven with a temporary assignment on earth. What I do here will determine my rewards in heaven. This body will die, but our spirit will live on. I have realized that Parkinson's was not a punishment from God, but a display of His grace. Having Parkinson's brought me to the realization of God's pruning. He is more concerned with my character and my assignment than the illness that I'm going through. He is using it to bring out my best. But I must trust Him for strength. Our purpose on earth was never meant to be easy. We can't do it by our own strength. We must rely on God for spiritual gifts that make it easier. Without God, we can do nothing. I realize that God did not give me Parkinson's. The enemy afflicts us. He comes to steal, kill, and destroy. But God uses illness and disease for our advancement, to show all things work together for good. Satan tormented Job. God allowed it for a season. Life's tests can be your testimony. Whose pain do you feel? That is your ministry.

CHAPTER 64
A brutal day for Parkinson's

The weather was calling for up to six inches of snow. The air temperature was 24 degrees. I bundled up to go shovel. Usually, I help with five different driveways, but I'm not a spring chicken anymore. I'm 67, with a Parkinson Shuffle and a tremor. Our church also called for a 21 day fast, and I was on day five of the fast, weak from not eating. What used to take thirty minutes now takes me hours. I shoveled for ten minutes, then fired up the snowblower. My friend Tom from Wrightsville decided to pay me a visit to help with the snow removal. If he had not shown up, I would've been a real mess. I have a heater in my shed, so we went in there to talk after we were done. I was not feeling good. It didn't take long for me to excuse myself to go lie down. Thanks, Tom, for helping me today. I did not help with anybody else's driveway this morning, which is unusual.

Later in the day, as I felt better, I came out to help some elderly people. We had another two inches of snow. It looked like it was done. I helped three people get their driveways done. We worked together to accomplish this.

One was my 70-year-old cousin, Doris, who lives across the street. She stuck by my side to help me in whatever way she could. Partway through, she looked at me and said, "you look awful." I replied jokingly, "just don't tell anybody." She helped me get it done. I excused myself and went in to lie down. My legs and back were in excruciating pain. Why do I continue to help other people when it is so hard on me? If I have breath, I will continue to persevere.

Being a blessing to others does not have to cost you money. Eyes wide open, looking for opportunities to do what you physically can.

CHAPTER 65
One small gesture can change their day

After our men's group this morning, I was praying about which direction I was to drive. Nothing specific hit me so I just started driving. I wanted to do something new this morning. I stopped at a different grocery store. I walked around for ten minutes but did not feel anything spiritual. I exited the building. I thought, what a waste of time. I drove about a mile to the next grocery store that I frequent. I carried a gift card in my pocket in case I give one out before I buy more.

I parked my truck and saw my opportunity this morning. I knew it in my heart, but I turned and walked away. As I did, my heart got heavier. I turned around and started to approach her. I offered to take her cart. She thanked me but looked distraught. I said, "I know you are done shopping for today, but I would like to bless you with a $50 gift card for the next time you shop here." "Seriously?" She replied. "You have no idea what that would mean." "Maybe I don't, but I know God does!" "Wow, this is incredible, you're an angel." I silently prayed for her as I walked to the store.

Now I know that the previous stop that I made today was not a setback, it was a setup, so that I would be right on time! It was not a waste of time, but a time of preparation for God's timing to unfold.

Today I bought four gift cards, and it didn't take long to give them away. The first recipient was already done shopping and headed out the door. I asked her if I could talk to her, and she stopped to listen. I felt an instant connection. The Holy Spirit will do that. I told her how I bless people with cards for grocery purchases. She wasn't sure that she needed one, so I gave her the opportunity to take the card and keep it for next time or give it away to someone else who could use it. She opted to give it away. "What is your reason for doing this?" she asked.

I told her, "Our pastors say that we are to 'make a difference' in our community. The Bible says, 'But do not forget to do good and to share, for with such sacrifices God is well pleased.'"

"I knew it! You love Jesus. I am really touched by what you do." With tears streaming down her face, she replied, "I will gladly give this to somebody in Jesus' name." She lives about a mile away and had been shopping there for many years. Now challenged to be a giver, she looked for someone to bless. Her name was Whitney, and it means "peaceful water." How fitting for such a beautiful child of God.

The stories that I can tell! I am blessed beyond measure. God promises to turn our mourning into dancing. Having Parkinson's disease, as debilitating as it can be, has become my new avenue for ministry.

Psalm 30:11 AMP

You have turned my mourning into dancing for me; You have taken off my sackcloth and clothed me with joy.

CHAPTER 66
Ministerium meeting today

I was ready early. As I was heading to the meeting and passing a supermarket, I heard, "turn here." I safely made a lane change and entered the parking lot. As I was looking for a place to park, I came to a stop sign. On my left was a young lady with a toddler. I thought, "right place, right time?" I rolled down the window. "Good morning," I said. "I am looking for somebody to bless today. Would you like to be that person?" She asked, "I'm not sure, what's the catch?" "No catch, I would like to bless you with a gift card for this store. You were at the right place at the right time. So, I am offering it to you." "Ok," she said, "are you sure?" "I am positive! God led me to this stop sign with you standing here. Right place, right time!" She smiled and received the card. How I love what I do!

Sometimes I get insight into how people are struggling. God will sometimes give me specifics. I sold some rods and reels that I don't use anymore. It was the reason that I had $300 cash in my pocket. When I have cash, I usually pray and ask God what I should do with it. Last night a young pastor's face flashed through my mind. At that time, I thought I would probably see him tomorrow at the ministerial meeting. I felt strongly that I should give him all $300. I didn't know how to go about it. I left it up to God to set it up.

I arrived early at the Ministerium meeting. I sat in my truck, praying for the meeting. The first young pastor and his wife showed up. I followed them in. We had about twenty minutes until the next person showed up. Totally God orchestrated. I told him that I would like to talk with him privately while his wife was getting ready for the meeting. I said, "yesterday, God told me that finances are tight with you right now. I'd like to give you $300 cash, as God instructed me to do." With tears in his eyes, he said, "I just prayed about that this morning."

God's word says, "While you are still praying, the answer is on the way!"

Luke 12:12 ESV
The Holy Spirit will teach you in that very hour what you ought to say.

CHAPTER 67
Time to have church!

We had a good men's meeting this morning even though it was just the two of us. It really gets more personal when you can share one on one. I was fired up this morning with the things that God is doing in my life. I have been digging deeper into the word. My prayer life has increased immensely. Getting a chance to share this with somebody means the world to me. Our discussion was intense and invigorating. It's amazing how God will test us right after we talk about things. Like generosity. It seems like God has a sense of humor when He tests us, but I know it is for a reason. As the men's group ended, I got a call from a friend who was sitting at a nearby gas station with his vehicle's gas tank empty. He left his wallet at home. I said I would be there in a few minutes. This is what church is all about!

Hebrews 6:10 NIV
God is not unjust; he will not forget your work and the love you have shown him as you have helped his people and continue to help them.

I visited an old friend who was struggling with bone cancer. He recently fell and broke his hip and femur. I have been aware of his cancer condition for three years. I've seen him lose a lot of weight. He is just a shell of a man now. It is heartbreaking. I badly want to lay my hands on him to be healed. He had a brother and sister pass away from other types of cancer. He's ready to go. I've tried to share my faith with him over the years, but he has just not been receptive.

After that I needed some God time! Ministering can be exhausting. I needed to be refreshed and refilled. I went down to the river to inhale God's majesty. The view was spectacular, with the bright sun and a cloudless sky. Let all His creation sing His praise and show off His glory. I prayed while enjoying the view and then I took some pictures.

Next on my list was the Mount Joy Food Bank, listening to their needs and concerns for the upcoming holiday. Spam! They could use lots of spam. Things for baking cookies, cakes, and brownies. Turkey stuffing, and cranberry items. Ketchup, mustard, mayonnaise. Tuesday I will buy as much as I can for a Wednesday drop off. I said this before, and I will say it again: there was a time in my life when I needed the support of a food bank. I was ill for two years. No income, and debt piling up. God healed me and put me in a job position that eventually paid off all my debt. No bankruptcy! Now I give back, so others can benefit.

Matthew 25:35-36 NIV

For I was hungry, and you gave me something to eat, I was thirsty and you gave me something to drink, I was a stranger and you invited me in, I needed clothes and you clothed me, I was sick and you looked after me, I was in prison and you came to visit me.

CHAPTER 68
Dealing with vertigo today: the good, the bad, the ugly!

The Good:

Last night's Legacy banquet was awesome! The message was phenomenal. What a great story about PC's father. I now understand why so many gifts are unimportant to me because I love to give.

Before I met my wife, Karen, I lived week to week. If I had extra money, I would share it. What is the point of having new shoes if someone else is going hungry? My signature trademark was worn out shoes. Twenty-four years ago, I married someone who brought balance to my life. She taught me how to have a positive bank account and still be generous. Thanks to her, and God's principles, we can be legacy givers. What a tremendous freedom to not be in debt.

The Bad, the Ugly:

I knew the risk that I was taking being in a high decibel environment for over two hours. With a history of vertigo, I knew that it could get ugly. When I woke up this morning, it sounded like swarms of locusts drilling inside my head. The exposure was too much! My first thought was to seek prayer. If I could just get to the men's group, I could be healed. It was a struggle driving to the men's group. I should've known better. Was it stupidity or faith? I badly wanted to be healed.

When I got to the meeting, I got out of the truck and staggered horribly! My balance was off. My nausea was reaching its peak. I knew I had 20 to 30 minutes before it would be unbearable. I excused myself and went home. Praying all the way, Father, please remove this from me, so I can minister. I reached my driveway, and my entire world was spinning right then. Hoping I wouldn't stumble on the concrete steps, I managed to open the door and call for my wife. She graciously helped me in but had to leave for work. She was having a near impossible situation at work that needed attending to. Now, it was a matter of sleeping to avoid the agony. I slept for over four hours. I had nausea and vomited. That's the ugly part of the story. It's amazing what the body can do to restore itself.

His mercies are new every morning! Father, I accept them. I share this because my struggles are real! Yet somehow, I manage to push through. He is such a powerful and personal God. While He is comforting me, He is exhorting another. At the same time, He is admonishing or blessing someone else. He is God to over eight billion people with the ability to meet every individual need.

CHAPTER 69
Prune, stretch, repeat!

I was having a rough morning with vision and balance. I was trying to put a game plan into place for the day. That must have made God laugh. I had it all planned out, where to go first, then I had to scratch that plan. Then I heard; here is what I want you to do: head to Manheim. I thought to myself, that is doable. I can go to the grocery store and pharmacy in Manheim. Halfway there, I heard "turn here," and I was a little grieved in my spirit because that was not what I planned. But I have learned to check my attitude and readjust. God is up to something! I ended up at Manheim Tire. God takes me back there occasionally to show His goodness. The owner's wife really likes my zucchini bread. I dropped some off with her. We talked about my Parkinson's and some new strategies for the tremor. We talked about business and hiring employees. Then God nudged me to tell her to send us a text anytime that she wants prayer. God is stretching me! She thanked me for the offer and said it's nice to have people you can turn to when things don't make sense.

Just down the road is the Dollar Tree. I will stop there and get food for the food bank. I can get a full cart of supplies for around $100. I priced it out one time, almost three times the price if I purchased elsewhere.

When my cart was full, I headed to the register. Someone got behind me with one item. Someone behind them had three items. I let them go ahead of me. Timing is key. It was my turn with nobody behind me, so we started ringing up the items. Just as I started, another line formed behind me. I could hear them talking. One was calming the others by saying, "he does this a lot. He buys for the needy." The next thing I knew, she grabbed a cart and started putting my bagged items into it. Now we had several people excited about what they could do to help. One was bagging, one was filling the cart. Others were talking about how great it is to help people. I was just wondering in my mind, how many people did I affect here in this store? Another one opened the door for me, while another one told me how awesome it is to see somebody helping the needy.

After I loaded everything in my truck, I took the cart back inside the store, where they prefer to have it. Inside, I saw a young mother with three children enjoying their shopping time. I asked them where they would like to eat lunch today. I grabbed a handful of gift cards out of my pocket and gave her a choice of six different places. She chose McDonald's and was excited that she didn't have to make lunch. They thanked me with huge smiles on their faces. Kids dancing in the aisles because they're going to McDonald's! A simple act of kindness, changing the atmosphere.

About two hours later, I felt like I should head to Chick-fil-A to get some gift cards. I got about halfway there and heard "turn here." Seems to be the theme for today, not my will, but Yours, Lord. I ended up in a traffic jam, wondering if I made the right choice. Again, timing is key! I failed to remember that. As I adjusted my attitude, the traffic started to move. I was now getting close to my chiropractor's office. I knew I had some zucchini bread leftover, so I stopped to give some to them. The receptionist is always glad to get some bread. I stayed long enough to talk to the chiropractor for a few minutes, another strong Christian man in my life. We are always glad to encourage each other in the faith. I'm so blessed to have good people in my corner.

I was trying to figure out the quickest way to Lancaster from here. I was going to go straight and then turn right on route 30 E. I got to the traffic light and God said, "turn left, I want you in Columbia." A left turn it is! I started thinking, now that I'm in Columbia, I feel like I should stop at the Sheetz gas station and pick up a few gift cards and maybe fill someone's gas tank. I'm always looking for opportunities at the gas station. There's usually somebody who's in need. I bought $200 worth of gift cards at $25 each.

I felt like I was supposed to drive towards the dumpsters at the old Kmart Plaza, thinking to myself, maybe there's a homeless person there.

As I pulled into the parking lot, I saw a guy on a bicycle leaning over to pick something up off the road. When I circled around the parking lot, he was still there. I knew this was it. I pulled up beside him and asked if I could buy him a warm meal. Without hesitation, he replied, "yes, absolutely." We were next to Wendy's, so he chose a Wendy's gift card. We talked for about 20 minutes. He thanked me for the gift card and asked if he could pray for me. "I want to thank God for sending you." He actually had a small Bible, and he read some scripture to me. Then he asked if there was anything he could do for me. I said you already did. You allowed me to bless you as God instructed me to do. Then I asked him where he stays at night. "In the fields near Sheetz gas station." Sometimes they give him free coffee to keep warm. So, I gave him one of the Sheetz gift cards. I also handed him a goodie bag that Karen had put together. They contain handwarmers, cotton gloves, a bottle of water, snacks, and a McDonald's gift card. This was Karen's idea so she could give to the homeless walking the streets of Lancaster.

God says, "I did not call you to 'stay,' but I called you to 'go' into the world to be my hands and feet. Take my plan of salvation to the world. Be faithful in going where I send you. I will provide the harvest."

From an early age I wanted to be a preacher in the church. Now, my calling is not to preach to people who are well fed spiritually, but to take it to the streets where they are physically hungry and spiritually malnourished, and even those who are physically and spiritually imprisoned. Look for those who are being released from prison and need help getting set up in society.

Luke 14:23 BSB

So, the master told his servant, go out to the highways and hedges and compel them to come in, so that my house will be full.

Isaiah 61:1 ESV

The spirit of the Lord is upon me, because the Lord has anointed me to bring good news to the poor; He has sent me to bind up the broken hearted, to proclaim liberty to the captives, and the opening of the prison to those who are bound.

CHAPTER 70
More pruning

Welcome to the inner turmoil of necessary endings.

"Too often, as bad as the results of not pruning can be, we still persist in avoiding it because it involves fear, pain, and conflict. Yet to succeed, we must be pruned. How does that make you feel? Conflicted?"

This quote is from a book called *Necessary Endings* by Dr. Henry Cloud. This book helped me realize the necessity of pruning. There are things that I used to do that had to come to an end. How do you move on with the calling of God if you're doing your own thing? He's always calling us to something better.

Years ago, I wrote the following encouragement to a young man who was considering entering the mission field. It helped him realize that he had to put his life aside and put God in the forefront. That story recently came up while I was writing this book. It was now an encouragement to me. It's funny how I wrote it for someone else, only to bless me years later.

Kyle, it is OK to do what you want to do, until it's

time to do what you are meant to do. Most people don't understand who you are and what your talents are, let alone what you are called to do. Some things in your life are the result of your own hand, but most things are not. Have the courage to change what you can, and trust God for what you cannot change! We all have our crosses to bear, and on your knees will be where you find the strength to carry yours! Don't pray for the mountain to be removed. Ask God to give you the strength to climb it. Strength comes from climbing. Strength comes from resistance.

You can change the course of someone's life by sending them a note of encouragement.

CHAPTER 71
I must speak of the goodness of God!

I was working on my "honey do" list. My wife asked me to run to the post office. Some envelopes were time sensitive for mailing. Before I knew it, (God's timing) I was parked at the SKH grocery store. We needed distilled water for the humidifiers. Within a minute of entering the store, my attention focused on a middle-aged woman at the food bar. I heard the whisper "give her a card." She looked at me, then started walking away. I prejudged and walked the other way. The timing was not right. I felt it, the time was not yet.

Then I saw a mother telling her daughter that she could not have cupcakes. She put them down, then picked them up again, hesitating. While she had them in her hand, I placed a gift card on top of them, "I would like to buy them for you." Mom and daughter are now smiling. I continued down the aisle. There was an older gentleman with two items in his cart. I handed him a card. He replied, "why me?" I looked him straight in the eyes, and said, "why not you?" Before he had a chance to accept, or reject, I was giving another card to someone else. She was excited about receiving one.

Then I saw the lady from the food bar. She was now with her husband. Now was the time to give them a card! Now I understand. When I saw them about ten minutes later, they were all smiles, and still thanking me.

The cashier was very attentive. She was bursting at the seams when she saw me. While waiting in line, I turned to the lady behind me. She had a beautiful dessert in her cart with a few other things. I slid the card on top of the dessert and said, "this is for you." I am so surprised at how a small gesture can bring out a smile in people. We talked for a few minutes until it was my turn to check out. Then the cashier chimed in, "what an incredible man! He's always blessing somebody." She knows from experience. I had reached out to her about a month ago. I enjoy her sweet spirit. What a beautiful child of God. Her name is Margie, which means "Pearl" or "natural gem with many facets." How fitting!

Next, I will go to the post office. I have a way of getting side-tracked!

CHAPTER 72
Just be a blessing!

I had eight gift cards of various amounts, usually giving the higher amounts to bigger families. I was thrilled by today's events blessing three families and several elderly. I'm at the point where I don't write them all down. But there was one in particular today that melted my heart. An elderly lady was getting a salad from the food bar. She was ready to put it in her cart when I slid a card on top of her salad box. "I would like to buy you lunch today." Pondering it for a moment, as to what just happened, she said, "you don't have to do that." "But I want to. I want to be a blessing to you." With tears meandering down the beautiful sculpture of her aging face, she pulled me in for a hug and said that nobody had ever done that for her. I can't imagine going through life without receiving generosity.

CHAPTER 73
Cashiers are getting involved

As I entered the grocery store today, I saw a lady with an empty cart. Almost bumping into me, she realized it and apologized. She said that her mother-in-law recently passed away and she was in a hurry. We briefly talked about personal ministries and then she went her way. I had time to get enough information to pray. Listening is key! I try to hear what the needs are, so I can pray better. If you just give people enough time to relax and talk, you can be privy to their world. You can affect change just by knowing how to pray.

As I turned, I was facing a young family enjoying one of those fancy carts. She did not have many items in her cart yet. I offered her a gift card towards her purchase. Speechless, just a smile, priceless! Sometimes not much is said. A simple smile or thank you is enough.

I approached a young mother with two children as she was putting groceries on the conveyor belt. She was gracious for the gift card that I placed in front of her. Without hesitation, she started to tell me that her son was sick at home. I was just glad that I could help. I asked her son's name and I assured her I would be praying throughout the day for her son's healing. Through the tears, she said thank you, while reaching deep for a smile. Her daughter looked thrilled, so I asked if she likes to eat at McDonald's. Without hesitation, she softly said yes. I gave mom two gift cards to go out to eat.

One of the cashiers approached me today, elaborating on stories from gift cards. She was telling me that I gave a large amount to a family a few days ago. When she was done with her groceries, she passed the balance to the lady behind her. She didn't have many groceries and did not use all the money that was on the card. She passed it to the lady behind her. The cashier was so excited about the generosity of people.

Repeatedly, I am blessed by the cashiers telling me stories that I would otherwise have not known.

CHAPTER 74
Whose plans am I executing?

I had a 5:30 pm appointment in Lititz today. 'My plan' was to leave home at 4:00 pm. I was stopping at the Dollar Tree to get some more food for the Elizabethtown food pantry.

At 2:30 I felt the nudge to "go now." I'm thinking, "say what? That's a lot of wasted time." But I've learned to trust. I grabbed my things and started driving. I knew God was up to something. Timing was key.

My grocery cart was full, so I headed to the checkout. The lady ahead of me had crafts to make Easter baskets. I was curious. She told me she had three kids who were making baskets. I offered her three McDonald's gift cards, one for each basket. She was very thankful. Then I thought that mom should have one too. She declined and told me to give it to the cashier. The cashier declined and said, "nobody can help me now."

"Please tell me more, why can't anybody help you?" Abrasively she said, "I just found out that my car repair will be $600. I just put $1,400 into it before Christmas. I don't have that kind of money right now!"

Now I'm thinking, "God what should I do?" I didn't really need an answer. I emptied the cash out of my pocket and gave it to her. "This is a good start," I remarked as I loaded my cart. This left her stunned and speechless.

I took the groceries to my truck. In my heart, I felt like I wasn't finished. I grabbed a business card for a trusted mechanic friend. I called him and told him I would send a customer over and I would help with the bill. I was taking the cart back inside when I noticed her exiting the building to go home. Had I waited another hour to leave home, I would have missed her altogether. So, I gave her the business card and asked her to take the car to them as soon as possible. I told her that I would help with the bill. I suggested that she provide half the money, and I would take care of the rest. She could not understand why a stranger would do that. I told her God knew her situation and sent me to help. We talked some more about God's goodness, and how much He cares for her.

With all this in mind, I still had another 90 minutes before my next appointment. There is a Giant nearby. I went over to get gift cards for future events, since I had just given away the rest of my McDonald's cards. As I was coming out of Giant with various gift cards, I noticed that I still had an hour left before my appointment. I saw four cars parked in the back of the parking lot. As I drove towards them, I saw somebody sleeping in one. I approached cautiously. I noticed the window was down. I asked the young man if he was hungry and gave him a choice of restaurant cards. "Oh, wow," he said as I gave him four of them. Then we talked about how long he had been there. (He spent the entire winter sleeping in his car) I told him that God had me leave home early so I would have time for this encounter. I assured him that God has his back. He recently started going to church in town and someone told him that God will provide a job if he would just ask. He starts his new job this week! I gave him enough cards to get started, to make it through to his first paycheck. I know where he stays, so I will check up on him.

God's timing is awesome. I just had to listen. I could've stayed home and missed all these opportunities.

What will you do today? Whose life will you change?

CHAPTER 75
Having fun with foreigners

I was in Columbia yesterday for a men's meeting. We meet at 7:00 AM Friday mornings. We had a great time discussing the Sunday sermon. I took some photographs of the Wrightsville bridge before our meeting, so I could get pictures with different shades of light. I decided to go back down for more pictures once the sun came up. It's always interesting to get a shot of the sunshine peeking through the clouds. I was on the river's west shore in Wrightsville taking pictures while the sun was rising in the east. Too many clouds. I was hoping for that one special shot.

While I was there, I met a family from Quebec, Canada. They were staying overnight in their camper. I gave them gift cards for food and gas. They were a long way from home, so I decided they needed kindness as they journeyed. We talked for an hour, as I took pictures of their family for their memories. I got some good pictures of their camper and the kids at work. Or should I say at play? I assured them that I would be praying for them while they travel.

I can only imagine what an adventure in heaven would be like.

The next day, at the same place, I met people from Belgium. They were traveling in the United States for one year and then heading home. In two months, they will be shipping their camper back to Belgium.

I cannot imagine their adventure, but maybe I can relate. This has been quite an adventure with Parkinson's. What started out as what I thought was a death sentence has become one of the greatest journeys in my life as I learn to reach out to people who are hurting. Karen and I went from impacting two families a month, to now sometimes five families a week. We applied Christian principles from the Word of God.

1 Chronicles 29:15 NLT
We are here for only a moment, visitors and strangers in a land. Our days on earth are like a passing shadow, gone so soon without a trace.

CHAPTER 76
Driven to success

At age 16, after my father died, I was quickly thrust into being head of the household. I would go to school for four hours, then work for five hours before returning home to work some more in the evenings. I had an apartment, a vehicle, and insurance to pay. I threw myself into things and became a type A overachiever.

I taught myself how to play drums while traveling with different Gospel music groups over the years. In the meantime, I was leading a youth group and teaching Sunday school. I was confused about my path in life. I was trying to walk as a mature Christian, but I was still a baby trying to make up for a lost childhood, hitting the road of life at 90 mph.

I found a small church in Marietta, PA that needed a drummer. I was given positions that I was not worthy of: music ministry, teaching Sunday school, youth group, and front-line ministry positions. I was entrusted with souls, yet I was a spiritual baby myself. The church grew from forty people to about one hundred and twenty. Our church stepped out in faith to build a new building. We could no longer house that many people in our old building. Thank God for the increase.

I was married at age twenty and kept pursuing carpentry as my business career. I volunteered to take my wife to Chester city to help grow an inner-city church that just started. I felt like I had an apostolic anointing on my life. Help start another church, I can do that. We had about forty people and grew it to about 100 when we left a year and a half later. I was an assistant to the pastor, but not a pastor. I was a youth leader, but not a youth pastor. My push to have the title of pastor brought great opposition and many struggles. I took a Bible course to get me there but ended up nowhere.

Throughout my adult life, I continued as a carpenter, blueprint drafting technician, electrician, plumber, roofer, siding, concrete, and jack of all trades. With my love of fishing, I started competing with other anglers, proving myself to be talented. I started entering higher brackets, where the competition was fierce. Over the years, I spent a lot of money on tools, trucks, boats, and fishing tackle.

My divorce came after twelve years of marriage, and I kept pushing myself to be something, but I did not know what. I was so driven but had no long-term goals. I raised my oldest son until he was 17 years old and graduating from school. I also participated in ten short term mission trips. I became a massage therapist, studied anatomy and physiology. I attended two years of Bible school and Preaching 101. I was constantly throwing myself into work projects and people, wanting to do more for the kingdom. I was achieving highly at everything I set my hands to do. I had many trophies on the shelf, but few trophies in the kingdom. I received awards from townships for my building projects while I was in business renovating houses.

I had been single for twelve years since my divorce. While I was on one of my mission trips, I met Karen, a divorced/single lady, with the same heart and passion that I had for people. We married shortly thereafter. As a blended family, the struggles were great. We were both goal-oriented and business minded. That seemed to compound our issues. Keeping God at the forefront kept our commitment real. The gossip at the time of our marriage was that we would not make it! What kind of encouragement is that from Christians? Karen and I were determined to make our marriage a success. After all, we were both type A personalities. Despite our struggles we always had time to hold hands and go to church. Tithing was not a question, it was necessary! At least we agreed on something.

What are we working for? What are we building towards? We have our own little kingdom. How does that work towards eternity? Am I leaving a mark or am I leaving a legacy?

In this story I mentioned all the things that consumed me. I was grasping for accomplishments leaving no room for God's purpose in my life.

When you are driven to succeed, somebody loses!

CHAPTER 77
I want to do good things, but I don't have time!

Ask yourself what steals your time? Besides your medical condition, if you have one, what consumes your life?

I was so driven to success that there was no room for God to entrust me with more. I had to reach a point where I crumbled so I could see His purpose for my life. Although some things in our lives may not be morally wrong, they weigh us down from running the race. These things keep us from devoting ourselves to God, the way that He would want us to. Some people have an absence of power because there is a lack of consecration to God. He wants to put power in your hands, but He can't if your hands are full of other things.

If you want power, you must lay down your will. Do we know how to have a commitment with Christ without having to control His will for our lives? Are we laying down the brass knuckles, and the chains and bats that we brought to the fight? Seriously, we may be trying to fight the mountain or circumstance that God meant as a character builder. We fight it, and we ask God to remove it, instead of asking God to come in to show us how to navigate it!

God will never approve our plans over His will. But I just can't do it on my own! That's right. God has made your calling beyond your natural ability! What God created you to do is impossible for you to do on your own. God, on purpose, made your calling beyond your natural ability so you can't boast. You can't accomplish your calling without your gifting. Your gifting is supernatural and given to you by God. Only then you can do what you were called to do!

Jeremiah 33:3 NKJV
Call on me and I will answer you and show you great and mighty things, what you do not know.

We have the power!

When you go into a place to speak, you are not just saying words. There is power, there is life, there is vitality in what you say. You bring a spiritual light and spiritual power that was not there before.

When a worship leader takes the stage to sing, the words coming out of his mouth bring power and light that was not there before. Power should penetrate everyone that it lands on. Everyone that hears it should be affected.

When a speaker walks into a room where people are talking, the power of his presence should be felt.

Conversations should cease. There should be an anticipation of what he is going to say.

Professors, when they walk into the room, command silence to those who know the teacher's words are powerful. They know they are going to learn something.

That's the kind of power we should exude! The power of the Holy Spirit.

Luke 24:49 ESV
And behold, I am sending the promise of my Father upon you. But stay in the city until you are clothed with power from on high.

CHAPTER 78
Jesus, to John the Baptist

There are times when I wonder if I will ever get my healing from Parkinson's. Paul asked God to remove the thorn, and He did not. Jesus asked the Father to remove the cup, but the Father sent ministering angels to help fulfill His purpose. The cup was never removed. Timothy was not healed from his stomach issues. Paul told him to drink a little wine to comfort his stomach. This is what Jesus told John the Baptist, through John's messengers: get your eyes off not being released from prison and see what I am doing.

Sometimes we must surrender what we think is our right to know, so we have no choice but to walk by faith. Sometimes it is not for us to know on this side of heaven, but to trust the One who does know.

Is your thorn your place of fulfillment? Think about it. Paul wrote four books of the New Testament while sitting in a dungeon in prison, a place where he might have thought God had forgotten about him. This was probably one of the toughest times of his life, but a necessary place to fulfill his purpose. Sometimes called the Prison

Epistles, the letters of Ephesians, Philippians, Colossians, and Philemon were written from prison and yet they deal with some of the most liberating concepts imaginable.

God brought Joseph out of prison and God brought Paul into prison. Both fulfilled their destiny.

Just as I was finishing this page, my wife handed me a book from Max Lucado. *God's Roadmap for New Beginnings*. Here is what he says: "God would prefer we have an occasional limp than a perpetual strut, and if it takes a thorn for Him to make His point, He loves us enough not to pluck it out! There are times when the one thing you want is the one thing you never get. What if your request was delayed or denied? If God says 'no' to you, how will you respond? If God says, 'I've given you my grace, and that is enough,' will you be content? Content: a state of heart in which you would be at peace if God gave you nothing more than He already has. Test yourself with this question: what if God's only gift to you was His grace to save you? Would you be content? What if His answer is, 'My grace is enough,' will you be content? From heaven's perspective, grace is enough."

Many people and things have a role in influencing your life: talking to the Father in prayer, the Bible, godly books, pastors, teachers, spouses, friends, and more. If you focus on your condition, it will bring you down. Take your eyes off your condition. Reach out to someone who is hurting, someone that you can comfort. As you lift others up, you yourself will be lifted up. God says in your weakness, you will be made strong.

I'm living that life! Although Parkinson's may slow me down, I still have purpose in helping others in need. You can too, no matter what your condition. Eyes wide open, everybody looking around, what do you see? It's your move!

CHAPTER 79
The church message hit home today!

I've bounced back from a lot of things over the years. In the mid-1990s being exposed to chemicals almost ended my life. Doctors had no answers, letting me suffer without any hint of how to deal with my problems. I was so ill, I missed two years of work. Because of my income level, I could not get food stamps or government assistance. I accrued a massive amount of debt. God eventually led me out, healed me, and restored me with a job. Within a few years, I was debt-free. Resurrection power! Although devastating, I recovered.

From the valley to the mountaintop, I rode that mountain top for years. I've had many highs and lows throughout the years since, always bouncing back from the lows.

In 2021, there was another attack. Or should I say series of attacks? I had Covid bad for eight weeks. After that, I was almost immediately diagnosed with Parkinson's. With that came a tremor in my dominant hand, growing worse over three years and now to the point of minimal usage of my hand. I've been in therapy to retrain it. I have developed hyperacusis hearing along with tinnitus and high-pitched squeals. Vertigo and Ménière's disease crept in with bouts of dizziness, nausea, and vomiting. How I wished the world would end. This has been one of the lowest seasons that I've ever experienced. But it doesn't stop there. I had a car accident where I was hit from behind. I have developed trigeminal neuralgia in my jaw with pain so debilitating I could only scream for relief. I dealt with a lot of pain over the years, but this was excruciating. Doctors told me I would need to have a molar extracted to remedy the pain. More pain on top of pain! My valley just hit a new low. I have asked God many times to remove these problems and heal me, only to be disappointed that they still exist.

I feel like my Christianity is being challenged. Why am I not healed? Am I in sin? Am I not right with God? Where are the answered prayers? I feel like I'm on a roller coaster, and I can't get off. I feel trapped with no way out. It reminds me of the story of Job in the Bible.

Now, on a positive note, if it had not been for these issues, would I be spending as much time with God? Why did it take all of this to get close to God? The truth of the matter is, I was just too busy! Now, due to Parkinson's disease I have more time on my hands, and I search the scripture for answers. But I'm still not healed. People asked me what I'm doing wrong because I'm not healed. I had no answers for them. Then today's message came: Having Peace in the Midst of Trouble. It was a new way of looking at my life of pain. I did seem to lose my joy over all this. Now maybe I can find peace again. Thanks to Pastor Curt for being bold enough to bring this message! I find comfort as I look back and thank God for the healings in my past, proof that He can do it. John 16:33 was in the message today. Four days prior to the message, I put that scripture verse to a picture of a person in a wheelchair, representing my health challenges.

John 16:33 NIV
I have told you these things, so that in me you may have peace. In this world you will have trouble. But take heart! I have overcome the world.

A special thanks to Pam Seaburg for her kind words and encouragement this morning, while we were visiting Columbia campus. Karen and I are blessed when we are in her presence. Pam, you are such an inspiration. Your words laid the foundation and created an environment for worship. Our time of worship prepared us for the word brought forth by PC. It's like having a brick-and-mortar foundation to build upon. Having peace in the midst of trouble: now that's a concept I can build on. Yes, I have troubles, and now I have scriptural proof that I can have peace while having trouble.

Message reference:
Advent, Hope Joy Love Peace Part 3 - Peace
December 17, 2023 • Curt Seaburg
https://victorychurch.org/resources/messages

I wake up each day, asking for guidance and purpose instead of asking for healing. I'm starting to ask for peace in the midst of trouble, hoping that someday the healing will come.

CHAPTER 80
Job suffered well

Job didn't blame God for his hardships. We are not to blame God. He didn't listen to his lame friends, who tried to explain why he was suffering. You make matters worse when you try to explain why God didn't heal. Don't make a theology of it just because your healing didn't manifest. And foremost, do not be that lame friend to someone else! We don't have the perspective that God has. We don't see things the way He planned them. Some things don't need to be explained. Some things we won't know on this side of heaven. We are limited in our understanding.

If God would be small enough for me to understand, He would not be big enough for me to worship!

Satan cannot touch us without God's permission. At what point did God say enough for Job? At what point does He say enough for you?

Could it be that the things that are frustrating you are the hand of God protecting you? God told Job that he would laugh again, and so will you!

Heavenly Father,

If today is not the day that I am healed, then send ministering angels so that I might carry out the task that You have for me today. Help me to fulfill the days that You have written for me. Amen

Psalm 34:19 ESV
Many are the afflictions of the righteous: but the LORD delivers him out of them all.

CHAPTER 81
The importance of Scripture, God's Word is His lifeline to us

Over the last two years, three scriptures are more prevalent in my life. They continue to reappear in teaching, preaching, and devotionals.

Proverbs 29:18 MSG
If people can't see what God is doing, they stumble all over themselves.

John 16:33 NIV
I have told you these things, so that in me you may have peace. In this world you will have trouble. But take heart! I have overcome the world.

Nobody is exempt from the weariness of life. No matter what age or season of life you are in, you can get weary.

Isaiah 40:28-30 NIV

Do you not know? Have you not heard? The Lord is the everlasting God, the Creator of the ends of the earth. He will not grow tired or weary, and His understanding no one can fathom. He gives strength to the weary and increases the power of the weak. Even youth grow tired and weary, and young men stumble and fall.

In John 16:33 trouble is part of the promise! Why should we be exempt? In Him we have peace. In Him we have strength. Or have you not heard? He told us these things to assure us. Digging deeper into His Word allows us to understand and prove His words. Reading it once, saying it doesn't work, and moving on, does not constitute digging deeper! Then if this doesn't work, the Bible doesn't work. And if the Bible doesn't work, His promises aren't real.

The Bible, the Word of God, is our lifeline. Grab on and hold on tight. You can't let go of a lifeline when you're trying to be saved. If you let go of the lifeline, who or what will save you?

CHAPTER 82
Adding great people to your arsenal of weapons

When I talk about Parkinson's disease, I speak from my level of experience. In no way do I put down or demean anybody else's medical condition! We all have our battlefields, our thorn in the flesh. Be aware of what God is doing through your struggles. Your test can be your testimony. How you manage your life through your condition will determine the level of how you help other people. How will you react if God chooses not to heal you? That has been my battlefield.

When there are too many people in your life, there is no room to add anyone who would benefit you. Sometimes there is no choice but to remove someone to make room for someone else necessary for your advancement. Getting to the next level is crucial to your ministry and for the kingdom.

I felt like God was removing people from my life that I held dearly. When you have Parkinson's, your world has been turned upside down. I understand now how even good people in your life may not be enough. You need the right people in your life, especially when you're on the battlefield, whether your battlefield is disease, cancer, addiction, depression, abuse, anything medical, or your fight against sin in your life.

About a year ago, I was sitting by a boat ramp resting after ministering to the homeless. I knew there was more to this day. I could feel that God was up to something. I started talking with a fisherman about his success on the water. His name is Doran. I had an instant connection with him. He became a person God wanted in my life. Doran is a Christian brother, full of life, full of scripture, not afraid to pray. One day he asked me what it means to fear God? I gave him my generic version, but even then, I was not satisfied with my answer. I had heard sermons on godly fear but was not sure that I was living it with understanding. One or two times a month I would dig into it. A little too deep? Well, maybe. It's like eating the whole smorgasbord in one meal. It can't be done. But I like it when people challenge me to go deeper with God.

Doran and his wife Amy have challenged my life in ways that they will never know. Reading Amy's book, *Love More* (by Amy Artman), allowed me to open up to the truth of my past and brought me to a point where I could share my current illness, past addictions, and my flaws with others. For me, as a friend, Doran's life has been rock steady, while Parkinson's takes me on a roller coaster ride. He sees the effects of having Parkinson's and without fail, he continues to pray for me.

Caution: be slow to anger when God removes people

from your life. He is making room for someone else that you need. Acknowledge His sovereignty and accept the changes that He brings. Then, do what you are called to do, and actively advance the kingdom.

When people are removed from your life, it is because seasons have changed. They served a purpose for an assignment. After that assignment is over, they are removed. I worked in construction for 40 years. There were times when we needed a scaffold to do a job. When that job was over, the scaffolding needed to be removed. It was no longer necessary, and it would interfere with the use of what we built. It had a purpose, but now it would be in the way and would be hard to navigate through the scaffolding to get inside. If God would not remove people after their purpose in your life is complete, it would interfere with the integrity of you fulfilling your purpose.

Proverbs 27:17 ESV
Iron sharpens iron, and one man sharpens another.

I said this elsewhere in the book, and it deserves repeating. Some people are a one-time thing, some people for a season, some for a lifetime. Although the removal is painful, it is necessary to propel you in your purpose. If they stayed, they would get in the way or hinder your effectiveness.

CHAPTER 83
My 2002 opioid addiction

Opioids: where would I be had God not intervened? I was taking eight pills a day, eight months after an L4/L5 spine fusion surgery. It was destroying my marriage. My heart became hostile territory, and Karen was no longer allowed in. We were only married for two years. I was no longer an encouragement. I could no longer breathe life into our relationship. I was mean and angry but did not know it. She finally confronted me about it. My life emotions were gone. Was I willing to see it? Was I willing to address it? This was a hard choice. I hated to see the resentment on my wife's face. Our love grew cold. I was no longer working because I was going to physical therapy. My prayer life grew dim. My fire for life went out. I waxed cold.

"God, help me fix this! I am about to lose everything." Little did I know how God would answer this. I called my surgeon and asked for a refill. He was three hours from leaving the office and going to Italy for two weeks. His secretary called me at the end of the day. She explained that he would not refill my prescription. He thought I was abusing it. I was down to my last pill. The next two weeks were a living hell! I went into withdrawal: sweating, freezing, shaking, crying. If there was ever a description for torment, this would be it! When my surgeon returned home, I was his first call. "Oh John, I am so sorry! I thought you were someone else asking for more pills. I don't feel that you are abusing pills. I will call in the script, pick it up myself, and bring it to you."

I was relieved to hear that, but now I am confused. I was on day thirteen of withdrawal. How many more days till it's over? He said, "the worst is over, you have about another week to break the addiction." "Let's roll with that," I replied. "How much worse could it get?"

It did get easier, but the emotions were still there. I had to learn to deal with the temptation of going back and learn how to cope with pain. After all, it was a major surgery. This was my chance to make it right. I asked God to help me.

For the next nine months, I fought the good fight. Six months of rehab for the back without meds. Finally, I was back to work for three months and doing well. My surgeon was impressed with my effort and my success. "No one has gone back to work in construction, after surgery like you had."

But I had a problem. My toolbelt sat directly over the screws that held my spine together while the bones fused. I needed more surgery to remove the hardware so I could wear my toolbelt. My surgeon assured me that "90% of the work is done. Rehab should be a short stint after removing the hardware. Then you will be good to go." "That sounds great to me. I love construction. I long to be productive again."

Long story short, there was a nerve trapped in the scar tissue. It was cut during the surgery. I spent the next eight years rehabbing my lower back. It was the best of times; it was the worst of times. How true. Now I was on another faith journey. I filed for disability. Little did I know that this was where a new ministry would begin. Another test, another testimony. Because of my trials, I could now see the hurt on people's faces and in their eyes. Go! Minister to the world. Yes, this could be where it really began, in 2002.

As bad as it was, it pales in comparison to the health challenges I now face.

CHAPTER 84
God's protection, I was not listening!

Having a notion or a feeling to turn here, instead of going the way you planned to go, may not always be for somebody else's benefit or somebody getting their prayers answered. It could be that it's about God's hand of protection on you. He could be taking you in a different way to keep you out of harm's way. He might be keeping you from being tied up in traffic longer than you need to be.

I recall the time I got a feeling of turn here when I ignored it. Three blocks later I was rear ended in an auto accident with about $8000 in damage to my truck. Too late to say, I should've listened! The damage was done. There was no erasing what happened. There are no do overs. Just learn from the mistake and move on. Now I had to deal with several weeks of inconvenience because I did not listen. It was the cross that I must bear for my decision. I must face the consequences.

Sometimes God tests your listening before He uses you on the next big thing. Be diligent and be faithful in listening.

Isaiah 30:21 ESV
And your ears shall hear a word behind you, saying, 'This is the way, walk in it,' when you turn to the right or when you turn to the left.

CHAPTER 85
So how do I make a difference?

What about neighborhood opportunities?

Some people want to be called to the world but fail to do what God called them to do for their neighbors. There are people who ask, "God, which country should I go to?" They ask, "Which ocean should I cross?" when God has been saying all along, "Why haven't you crossed the street to where I sent you?" If you walk around your neighborhood with your spiritual eyes open, you will find opportunities! Learn the names of your neighbors and remember them. Call people by name when you are walking down the street. It says to them that they are important. Ask what's up? Be ready for opportunities when they answer. It may not be that particular day. It could be a month from now or a year from now. Plant the seed. Be ready, you may have to react now! What is the Holy Spirit saying? Be in tune. Here are a few of my own personal examples.

An 80-year-old man said to me, "it would be nice if I had a handrail to hold onto while using my steps." I'm thinking, that's something I can do. So, I did it.

I was talking to another neighbor who was waiting for the men in her family to help her install a dog fence. I asked her to show it to me. I told her I would be back in ten minutes and take care of it. It didn't take long to do.

Another one needed pressure washing done. I have a power washer; I can do that.

Another neighbor had a stroke, so we volunteered to do her yard work.

Another neighbor has cancer, so I make meals for him.

Opportunities abound! In our neighborhood, Karen and I make it an adventure. We solicit help from other people to join us in projects. It makes it more fun, and gets it done quicker. It also allows you to get to know other people while they are helping.

CHAPTER 86
Why am I still here?

There is still Kingdom work to be done! I will keep planting seeds in hope of more harvest. With all my health issues, I wonder how long I can go on.

After sharing some things at the men's group this morning, I decided to make some detours on my way home, talking to people, planting seeds, and being an encouragement. And when I got home, I sat and wrote in my journal. I really enjoy it when I have divine appointments. On days that I don't have divine appointments, I choose to be generous to people. I've been texting with a young pastor. He cried as he told his wife about our encounter last week. He said he needed that meeting so badly. In this case, he just needed somebody to talk to. We were all wounded at one time or another. We should choose to be a healing salve to those who are wounded so they can heal faster.

The first thing people notice is my tremor. They give me a puzzled look. They tell me how I look good despite the fact. How should I look? Typically, I hear, John, you always have a smile on your face. It truly does show the presence of God in my life. But they usually don't have a chance to see the bad and ugly in Parkinson's. Without

God, I would surely want life to end. But knowing that once I step through that door to heaven, there will no longer be a chance for me to win another soul. There will not be a chance for me to help someone who is hurting or struggling.

I encourage you to do what you can now, because when your life is over, there is not another thing you can do here on earth. Make the most of your time here. Find your calling, and you will not regret it.

One second in heaven, and you will have all your questions answered! You will then know that God knew what He was doing with every situation in your life. You will know how He used pain to bring about your purpose and to build character in you. You will know whether the prayer was answered your way or His way. Either way, pain and pruning produces fruit. God gives us glimpses along the way, as well as answers of "yes" to help build our faith.

I remember the time I was healed of a damaged knee. I was healed instantly and without any recurrence for over twenty years. I had another healing that wasn't instantaneous. Over time God allowed me to be healed of a chemical sensitivity issue. I was exposed to chemicals as a youth while on the farm, and at different times through my adult years. I would avoid people and places that would trigger migraine headaches. I have seen healing in others, and I've had my own. These times strengthen my faith, but the questions remain for the unanswered prayers in my life.

You may not get your answer on this side of heaven, so while you are here, try to live with the mystery! Live life by faith, knowing that God has your back. After all, He is your rear guard.

Isaiah 58: 8 NKJV

Then your light shall break forth like the morning, your healing shall spring forth speedily, and your righteousness shall go before you; the glory of the Lord shall be your guard.

CHAPTER 87
Future story, His glory

God will use your present situation, in your future story, for His glory. "But I don't like my present situation!" It doesn't matter because you are in it. He's going to take you from where you are now and use it in a place where you are going to be in the future, to give you the opportunity to bring glory to His name.

God has never promised to explain everything to you on this side of heaven. But He has promised to use everything that comes against you for the good of Heaven.

Romans 8:28 NLT
And we know that God causes everything to work together for the good of those who love God and are called according to his purpose for them.

CHAPTER 88
Fighting the good fight, my point of view

Let me describe Parkinson's challenges. Most people with Parkinson's have a mask-like emotionless face, tremor of some kind, inability to move freely, freezing in place, and shuffling as they walk. Each person has their own set of symptoms. What shows up in one person may not show up in the next ten people. The combinations are endless. The same goes with the medications. Each person must figure out what works for them.

We found out that I could not tolerate the medications. I was allergic to the dyes and fillers that make up most of them. I had to find alternative methods to cope.

Exercise is necessary for Parkinson's people! If you don't know that by now, talk to your doctor about exercises and therapies. The right combinations of clean food, exercise/therapy, and good sleep will prolong your ability to stay mobile.

Why clean food? Parkinson's is a neurological disease. GMOs and food sprayed with pesticides are harmful to the nervous system. Most people with Parkinson's can trace back to pesticide or chemical exposure. Within the

Parkinson's community, the people who are doing their best have changed their diet and added exercise.

What kind of exercise/therapy? I tried to start with walking. That was not successful because of my shuffle and freezing. I could not pick my feet up high enough to walk, thus the shuffle. We bought a used *Theracycle* specifically for people with Parkinson's. I started at ten minutes a day, slowly working up to thirty minutes, and then sixty. The motorized pedals move your feet for you. The therapy bicycle reduces symptoms and improves motor function and mobility. Then I added walking to my routine. After that came resistance training with bands.

How much sleep? Typically, seven or eight hours of restful sleep. Restorative sleep is crucial to healing the body, nerves, and the mind.

I've had Parkinson's for about three years now. Yes, it's been challenging, including several different kinds of pain that I can't describe. I have spent many nights shedding tears due to pain and uncertainty. There have been mountains to climb, hurdles to jump, milestones to reach, and steppingstones to cross.

A special thanks to my wife, Karen, who has been my greatest support. Some days it's hard for me to do house chores. She works all day, then she comes home and finishes what I can't. I've been blessed beyond all measure. Our marriage has been built on teamwork. In 2011 she had an accident that crushed her lower leg/calf area. After several surgeries, skin grafts, and many months of rehab, she finally returned to work. I became a personal butler and nurse for almost 7 months. She dealt with her concussion for another four months. She believed for healing from the phantom pains and clarity in her mind. Many times, she would get lost while driving, and I would get a phone call from her, asking how to get home. I would have to talk her through it. Now she's totally healed! She's on the treadmill most mornings and makes it home from work every night. I learned a lot from watching her push through the circumstances.

Now that I have been diagnosed with Parkinson's, I can look back to somebody who persevered. She's my hero. Her test became her testimony.

I have noticed that the Parkinson's community has many people with knowledge and support. Make use of it!

There are several places in Lancaster County, Pennsylvania, where I found people with Parkinson's who were not in despair. When I get around people who are very active in their Parkinson's, I find that they do not let their condition steal their life from them. They keep active at places like Crush PD, Lititz Rec Center, Hartz Physical Therapy, and Penn Medicine LGH Neuroscience Institute. There are others, but these are the ones that I am familiar with. The whole idea is to keep your body moving. In my opinion, being active is the best answer: cycling, walking, boxing, and big movement therapy, just to name a few.

I also found help from Dr. Shayne Bushong at Lancaster Brain and Spine where he discovered that I had Nystagmus.

If you need therapy and can't leave home, Functional Freedom LLC offers in-home therapy services like Outpatient Occupational Therapy, Physical Therapy, and Speech Language Pathology. This is achieved in the comfort of your home.

info@functionalfreedomllc.com

CHAPTER 89
Fighting the good fight, another's point of view

In his book *Road to Recovery from Parkinson's Disease*, Robert Rodgers, PhD, says that there will never be a cure because the conditions that create the symptoms are multi-faceted. Each person's situation is entirely unique to them. That is why the symptoms vary so widely across individuals, and why the solution will be unique to each person. Trauma and toxins create havoc with the neurological system. Stress damages the neural connections. When you realize the complexity of the factors that caused the symptoms, it is easy to see why there is no single solution.

Davis Phinney, founder of the Davis Phinney foundation, says that it is a huge mistake to wait for a cure. Waiting means that you are not living. Embrace what you can do for yourself every day, whatever that might be.

Michael J Fox says, "I recognize how hard this is for people. And I recognize how hard it is for me. I have a certain set of skills that allows me to deal with this stuff.

I realized, with gratitude, optimism is sustainable. Find something to be grateful for, then you can find something to look forward to, and you carry on."

The Parkinson's Foundation publishes encouraging stories every month.

Everybody has a story. Whether diagnosed at 31 or 72, tremor or no tremor, fast or slow progression, feeling relief or anger at hearing the words "You have Parkinson's," every Parkinson's Disease (PD) story is different.

Every person who shared their PD Story with the Parkinson's Foundation has one thing in common: they hope their story might just help someone else. Each of the PD stories inspire us to keep making life better for people with Parkinson's. Let these testimonials remind you that you are not alone. We thank everyone who has found the courage to share their story with us and our global PD community.

Throughout every stage of Parkinson's disease, it is important to embrace every milestone.

CHAPTER 90
A word of caution as you learn to hear God's voice

Sometimes we get caught up in the way that God uses us repeatedly. We begin to develop a method. When we start to rely on that method, that's when we start to get in trouble. We start to miss the mark. Maybe God wants to do something new, using you in a new or different way. Don't get stuck. Be open to when God wants to shift gears. His desire is to take you to the next level, which requires more attention to the details.

If there is one thing you can count on with God, it is that you can never predict when He will change the course of your life and lead you down a path of blessings you couldn't imagine.

The prophet Isaiah proclaimed in Isaiah 43:19 that "God would do a new thing" in our lives, something we couldn't do ourselves. This thing would be impossible for people, but possible for God. The church is stepping into a new era. There will be new ways of doing things. God will be doing a new thing. His ways and methods may change, but He does not change.

CHAPTER 91
Raising the bar

After our men's group, I went down to the river to take some pictures. As I got there, my truck's fuel alarm went off, stating that I had less than fifty miles left of gas in the tank. Ignoring that distraction, I saw a man that I recognized. He was from the old neighborhood in Wrightsville. I stopped and talked to him for a while, catching up on neighborhood events.

I proceeded to take pictures of the sun shining through the trees, glistening off the water. I noticed a lady reading a book with her back to me. I spoke softly, trying not to startle her, just to let her know that I was there. Because I was taking pictures, she wanted to show me some pictures on her phone. They were of a beautiful sunrise, shining over the impacted ice on the river. I commended her for such gorgeous pictures. "You have an eye for this," I said. When she had put her book down to show me the pictures, I got a glimpse of the title! *The Demon's Sermon on the Martial Arts: And Other Tales.* My head told me to get as far away as I could! Run! But my heart said stay. God was up to something. We talked about Parkinson's and photography. I shared my testimony of finding my purpose through Parkinson's.

Raphaela started to tell me her story. She moved here, not too long ago, and had to start over with her martial arts, Kung Fu. Although she wanted to be with the advanced group, they would not allow her. She had to start all over again. It was so sad for her. She almost lost her zeal for the art, so she was reading this book. She felt held back. For her, to start over was a setback. I told her that it was a "set up." Her knowledge would overflow to the lesser trained students. She could have an impact on them in a way that the instructor could not. She pondered that thought with tears filling her eyes. I think God just read her mail! I continued to tell her about the samurai warrior that is on a path.

"The samurai warrior has a path. A path in which every day has a purpose. He does not set a goal in the future, nor does he try to figure out where the finish line is. He lives for today. No distractions from the past or future." "You gave me a lot to think about. Thanks for stopping and talking to me. You have no idea what you just did for me."

I felt the strength of my calling with such clarity. Maybe more than usual? And the Holy Spirit dropped this in my heart: "The call on your life does not get greater. Your call is the same. You're just listening at a different level now. You are anticipating great things, while you are tuning out the distractions."

Wait for it! Timing is key. God knew when and where I would be, to use me.

I decided to hold off on getting gas until I got to Mount Joy. I knew I could make it that far. I stopped at Giant to get some fruit before I got fuel. I had one $50 gift card to hand out. "Father, please show me who it's for!" Things feel different today. I sense the Divine appointments.

I got what I needed and proceeded to the register, where there was a new cashier today. She noticed my tremor and was being polite. Just as I finished paying, a mother with two children, now leaving, walked right by me. I motioned for her to stop and handed her the gift card. Total astonishment! Then I gave her son a McDonald's card. So happy about that! As she walked away, I did not notice that she did not leave the building. When I got to the exit, she was standing there waiting for me, full of questions. She said her name was Brittany. I told her that she was at the right place at the right time and God knew where she would be. I told her a little bit about my ministry. Then she asked where I go to church. When I told her, she said, "Oh, I know where that's at. I sent an email to the church to find out if they have childcare." I assured her that they did and invited her to join us. Brittany's family has been wanting to find a smaller church that had childcare. God had me there to answer her questions.

Before I left the store, I was summoned back in by one of the cashiers. She's in tears from what she just saw with the gift cards. "You touched my heart with what you do. It's so incredible." She gave me a hug and thanked me for making her day.

I heard my name, and turned around to another cashier, who was motioning for me to come talk. She told me of a story that touched her. A lady came through her line and talked about the gift card she received. Yet another story that I would not have known, except for the cashiers.

Now I went to my truck, sensing there's more. I put the cart back where it belonged. It dawned on me that I needed a card for my wife for Easter. Right next-door was the Dollar Tree. I entered, following a mother and daughter. The daughter looked at me and smiled. I offered her a McDonald's gift card. Rejoicing and jumping up and down, her and mother were happy.

I got my card and realized I didn't have any money on me. Just then, the mother walked up to me and realized I was struggling and asked, "how can I bless you today?" I told her I just came in for a card. She gently took the card and paid for it. God has my back! We hugged, I thanked her and smiled as I walked out the door. A lesson for me? It's about graciously receiving when somebody wants to bless you. Let them do what God asked them to do. Be humble and receive. I have noticed there are people who do not receive well when I offer. I'm OK with that, but they do miss a blessing. How do you handle it when somebody tries to bless you?

When I got home, I immediately sat down to journal before I forgot all of the details. Now, thinking about my first encounter at the river, I looked for that book on the Internet. When I read the notes describing the contents of the book, I realized that God did read her mail. I did not know that the book was about a samurai warrior, but God did, and He put His spin on it just for her.

This is what it said:

"This collection of parables written by an eighteenth-century samurai warrior is a classic of martial arts literature. The tales are concerned with themes such as perception of conflict and self-transformation."

Isaiah 61:1 ESV

The spirit of the Lord God is upon me, because the Lord has invited me to bring good news to the poor; he has sent me to bind up the brokenhearted, to proclaim liberty to the captives, and the opening of the prison to those who are bound.

CHAPTER 92
Giving encouragement

I headed to the river to take pictures this morning. I felt the nudge to turn right instead of left. I went to a different boat launch to take a few pictures. Who did I see? Raphaela! She was sitting with her friend Richard, waiting for the sun to peek through. All we got was a little drizzle and wind. It made things a little nippy. We talked for ten minutes and then I went to John Wright for more pictures.

The men's meeting was canceled for this morning, but I decided to wait for my friend George to show up. We will meet and talk anyway. George was running behind, no big deal. God is up to something. So, I decided to go back down to where I took pictures earlier. Raphaela was still there, just packing up and getting ready to go. I was hoping to talk to her alone but being with somebody today put a damper on it. I told her that I had a paper for her. She came to my truck and started to read it. I had written, "Raphaela, your greatest witness to people is your story. What happened to you in life cannot be minimized." I saw her starting to tear up and get choked up to the point where she couldn't talk. I gave her some more encouragement as she read the rest of the note. God has his hand on her. I looked her in the eyes and said, "you are something special. I haven't put my finger on it yet, but I know you're special. God has a plan for you." Now the tears were flowing. I knew it hit home. They pulled out of the parking lot as I was praying for them. Now waiting for George to show up at John Wright. Can't wait to see what God's doing with him.

Acts 15:31 ESV

And when they read it, they rejoiced because of its encouragement.

CHAPTER 93
God has my back

My divine appointment today was Tony, one of the elders of our church. He attends the Mount Joy campus. We bumped into each other at the Giant grocery store in Mount Joy. It was a great meeting. God knew that I was struggling with a few things and sent Tony to answer them. Tony did not realize it, so after I got home, I sent him a text:

Tony, I will try to make this brief. First, say thanks to your wife, Jen, for sending you to the store! She was following God's lead. You were obedient to get to the store. Only you didn't know it at the time. That's typically how it works. I told you that I had the prompting to 'go now' and I did. You were the reason I was there. But more important, I was the reason you were there. I needed direction on several things. You don't think you said much, but you did. The first thing you said was important to me, "it's time to be done writing your book, and place it in the hands of the professionals." Thank you for that word. I've been stressing over the little things in the book that someone else could be working on.

Then we talked about the Mount Joy campus. I've been struggling with not feeling connected to the campus. You encouraged me to search for ways to connect. You said, "we all need to make it into our campus, not just you." I have watched several people blossom since starting here. The stories that they bring back to me are awesome. Sometimes I get distressed from the medical issues that I am going through, and I can't see the big picture.

You followed that up with, "another way to feel connected is being involved in the community." That's one area that I/we have strength in. Our neighbors pull together to help each other. We have neighbors with cancer, strokes, death of a spouse, and failing health. We come together to help those who are in need. That all started when we had our pre-launch group here in the community. We had upwards to 18 people attending on a Sunday morning.

Thanks again, my friend. You were at the right place at the right time. You said precisely what I needed to hear. God used such a little thing to orchestrate you being there.

Isaiah 41:10 ESV
Fear not, for I am with you; be not dismayed, for I am your God; I will strengthen you, I will help you, I will hold you with my righteous right hand.

CHAPTER 94
Never tire of doing good

Karen's dentist is in Hummelstown. There is a Giant grocery store next to the Hershey Park roller coaster. I had two gift cards on me. I purchased four more inside the store.

The shirt logo on the first person I encountered was for Penn State Health. I thanked her for her commitment to the healthcare system, and the hours that she serves. She had a very tight window of opportunity to get her groceries. I further thanked her with a gift card and that made her day!

The second one was an elderly couple. They were so astounded that somebody would be willing to help them make ends meet. He was so kind and respectful. At first, he asked, "why?" I replied, "why not?" Then we chuckled.

The next elderly lady was puzzled. At first, she thought it was a gimmick until she saw the card with the amount on it. I think I saw a few tears. She didn't say much, but she didn't have to. Her eyes said it all.

The next story was so beautiful. She was a younger mother, who was grateful for financial help. After giving me a hug, she stated that she would like to do this ministry of helping somebody else someday. I pulled out another gift card, and said, "now is your time! You can give this card to someone else while using the one I gave you." She asked me why I would do that. My response was this, "when you give away this gift card, you will experience the same feeling that I have every time I hand a card to somebody. You will never forget it." Now she was all smiles and gave me a really big hug. She was on her way to fulfilling her destiny and spreading kindness.

As I exited the store, I had a chance to watch a young man remove a wheelchair from his car and help the passenger get into it. I greeted them when they got close enough, and asked if I could bless them with a gift card. There were tears of happiness as she accepted. The young man was speechless. It looked like he hadn't seen kindness in a while. I could tell it touched them both. She was not dressed for the chill in the air. I would've liked to have asked for her story. I could tell she was cold. As they went into the store, a young mother, with four children, was coming in my direction. I had two Burger King cards, and two McDonald's left to give away. I asked which restaurant they preferred and right away the older son said McDonald's. I gave her two gift cards. Everybody's happy!

I turned around to see an elderly man dropping off his wife for a hairdresser appointment. I immediately assisted in getting her out of harm's way with her walker. I waited with her till he parked the car and came to her side. We talked briefly as she slowly made it to the salon. I held the door open while they both went in.

All this is because of my wife having a dental appointment. I could have done nothing more than just wait. I'd rather look for a purpose!

2 Thessalonians 3:13 NIV
And as for you, brothers, and sisters, never tire of doing what is good.

CHAPTER 95
Mother's Day tribute

I've been feeling abandoned lately. Vestibular migraines and vertigo have been hindering my attempts. It's been a while since I gave away gift cards. Last time I tried, nobody accepted.

God gave me a new plan. I replenished my gift card supply and started my search. It seemed like there were a lot of elderly ladies here today. I started thinking about how I miss my mother. We had just celebrated Mother's Day, and that's a lonely day for me. Then I got an idea to give away gift cards in remembrance of my mother! God, that's brilliant!

I approached the elderly ladies one at a time. "In remembrance of my mother, I would like to give you a gift card for Mother's Day." Wow, nobody turned me down. I gave away twelve cards total at this location. What a change in the atmosphere. Cashiers were smiling and waving at me. They know what's up! I left there with a spring in my step.

I had an appointment in Centerville that I needed to get to soon. I did have a little time to spare, just in case. As I was driving, I saw something lying in the middle of the road; it was a pink kneeling pad that caught my attention. I turned around to pick it up and it was gone. It just vanished. I didn't see anybody stop for it. Was it really there? Did God use it just to turn me around?

Now I was headed in the wrong direction for my appointment. I looked for another place to turn around. I ended up at the parking lot of a laundromat. There were people inside. Was this the reason I turned around? Maybe opportunities to be a blessing?

I parked my truck and approached two ladies getting into their car. "Wait a minute," I stated, "you can't leave yet, I want to talk to you. Are you both mothers?" "Yes," they replied. "Great. How was your Mother's Day?" "Fabulous," one remarked. "That's awesome, I would like to make your Mother's Day even more special. I would like to offer you a restaurant gift card in remembrance of my mother who passed away several years ago." They chose from the stack of cards that I had and thanked me with a hug. Then I walked inside with more gift cards in hand. I approached all the ladies individually. I told them I was honoring my mother by handing these out. They all graciously accepted. I gave six cards in total at the laundromat. Excitement filled the air. Wow, what a day!

Happy Mother's Day Week!

The rain has a purpose here, before it returns to heaven. It nourishes the ground and makes things grow. It can go through many cycles before returning to heaven. It does not return void. It accomplished what was written in the book.

My mom returned to heaven, from where she was sent, with a purpose. At age 79, her purpose here was fulfilled, according to her book, which God before ordained.

Isaiah 55:10–11 MSG

Just as rain and snow descend from the skies and don't go back until they've watered the earth, Doing their work of making things grow and blossom, producing seed for farmers and food for the hungry, So will the words that come out of my mouth not come back empty-handed. They'll do the work I sent them to do, they'll complete the assignment I gave them.

CHAPTER 96
It's not a setback! It's a setup!

I marvel at all the opportunities that are out there. I had an issue to take care of at the post office. I just wanted to let it slide, but I felt drawn to take care of it, so I went in to deal with it. The person in charge was so apologetic. I'm taking advantage of the opportunity to offer forgiveness. That opened the door for my testimony. She noticed the tremor and knew I had Parkinson's. Her father has Parkinson's. She doesn't know what to do to help him. Also, her son has autism. She spent a lot of time trying to find ways to help him improve. She gave me her information and told me to contact her outside of business hours. We will be discussing how her dad can improve. As I was leaving, she stated that this was the best conversation she's had in a while, something to give her hope instead of bad news. I felt good about that.

I looked at my watch. Time to go! When I got to my truck, there was an elderly lady walking by with a Harley Davidson jacket on. Jokingly I asked her if she still rides. "Of course I do! I go as a rider. I do not drive anymore because my eyes are getting bad. I am losing my eyesight." I asked for her name so I could pray for her. She asked my name and said she would pray for me. I encouraged her to believe in God for healing. She sounded all choked up. I found out that I went to school with her younger brother. She was very interested in the book that I'm writing. "I won't be able to read it but if you put it on audio, I can listen." I started wondering how many others would like it on audio.

Also, I thought, if I did not have that postal issue to deal with, I would not have had these two opportunities. I'm glad I took care of it. So, the next time you think that you have a "setback" because of an issue, take a moment and think about it. It could be a "setup" for an opportunity.

My wife was not able to get ripe bananas this morning for baking, so she asked me to go buy some. I had gift cards in hand because there could be opportunities. As I got out of my truck in the store parking lot, a mother walked by with a completely full cart. My strategy was to retrieve her cart, using that as an opportunity to bless her with a gift card. "Wow, that's a lot of groceries!" "Yes, there's a lot of mouths to feed at home." I was trying to find the words to say next. "I know you're done shopping for today, but could you use a little help the next time you shop here?" Her jaw dropped in surprise when I gave her the gift card. Now I'm listening to her story while both of us are in tears. Her daughter was now crying because mom was crying. Mom had to explain to her that they were happy tears. So, I offered her daughter a Burger King card. Now she is happy too.

Inside the store, a young boy around eight years old was pushing his mother's cart. It was a struggle, but he was enjoying himself. I offered him a card of his choice and he picked McDonald's. Happy dance!

Being kind is an essential part of life. Being generous is a choice.

The real sorrow in life is getting to the end of it, and realizing there was more that could have been done! It's sad when you realize that you could have done more with your life but didn't.

CHAPTER 97
Ruby Jones

How about now? Singing someone's praises!

On April 11, 2018, I wrote this about Ruby Jones. I waited five years to share it with her. Why? So many times, we wait until someone is gone to sing their praises. Why not tell them while they are alive? Ruby, I'm sorry it took so long!

She is like no other! She will get down in the trenches with the best of them. She's not willing to see any be lost. To Ruby, R&R does not mean rest and relaxation. It could mean "Rummage and Recover." She will go into the trenches and search for those who are lost. She helps recover them so they can be whole. She is willing to go where nobody else will go! Over time, as I watched Ruby minister to people, I started to understand what Ruby was all about. Named appropriately, Ruby is unique. With a heart of gold and a body of flesh, you couldn't put two more opposites together to get better results. You press grapes, put them in bottles, let it age and you get fine wine. You put metals in the fire to remove the impurities for unique masterpieces. You put minerals under pressure, and you get precious stones. The end result is Ruby Jones.

I watched as people put her down and crushed her spirit. She has been through the mill, or you could say, through the wringer of life. No matter what is thrown at her, she still finds the strength to cry out to her Heavenly Father. God lifts her up again and again. If you look in the dictionary of heaven and find the word servant, it will read like this: there is none more precious than Ruby Jones!

Ruby is the founder of Perish No More Ministries.

Proverbs 3:15
She is more precious than rubies. None of the things you can desire are to be compared to her.

Isaiah 54:12
I will make your pinnacles of rubies, and your gates of sparkling jewels, and all your walls of precious stones.

CHAPTER 98
Mel Hurst

New concept? Thanking people while they are still alive! I got this crazy idea from a friend of mine who was dying of cancer. He came up to me one day and said, "why do we have to wait for people to die, to tell others of the good they did? Or that I meant something to them? I want to know, before I die, who I affected in a positive way. I want to know if my life mattered to people. He looked at Dave Parker, then he looked at me, "can you make that happen?"

Dave and I pondered that idea and started gathering people together to do just that. Over the next four weeks people came and testified to the goodness and generosity of Mel Hurst. We had some great crying sessions.

Dying of cancer is such a cruel way to die. But Mel wore it fashionably, making a mockery of the enemies attempt to minimize his life. Mel lived life to the fullest. Every day was an adventure for him. "Who can I meet today? Who can I help today? Who can I take to the next level? Who can I tell about God's love?"

Personally, I witnessed Mel in action. While we were on our way to a fishing destination, we stopped at a restaurant to eat. He asked the waitresses, "If the Man upstairs punched your ticket today, would you make it to heaven? Would you be ready?" I have seen the tears, and I have seen the rejection. Mel was doing what he was created to do.

Thank you, Mel Hurst, for touching my life in such a way that this is what I do now. I adapted to my own version of doing what you did. You planted seed in my life, and you will share the harvest in heaven. You are missed, but I realize that your time was up. Your days were fulfilled. The Man upstairs called you home. Fish on! <*})))))><

Whoever wrote the following statement must have known Mel:

"Life is not a journey to the grave with the intention of arriving safely in a pretty, yet well preserved body, but rather to skid in broadside, thoroughly used up, totally worn out and loudly proclaiming - wow, what a ride!"

CHAPTER 99
Turn me loose

I've been cooped up too long. I had been sick with vertigo for six days. I am now ready to go minister.

Now heading to a chiropractor appointment this morning. I was ready 45 minutes early. I decided to take a detour. I stopped at the supermarket and purchased five gift cards. A quick trip to the men's room, yes, I'm over 60; It's amazing how diversions get you to where you belong.

As I came out from the men's room, there was a Hispanic lady standing at the bargain shelf. I said hi to her and instantly felt drawn to talk to her. I asked her if the prices are affecting her. And if she could use some help financially for today's purchase. "Si," she replied, which means yes in Spanish. I was on mission trips to Mexico and Honduras. I handed her a $50 gift card with the receipt taped to the back of it. She saw the amount and her jaw dropped. "Gracias, God bless you." I replied, "Da nada, you're welcome, the reason I can do this is because God blesses me." She gave me a big bear hug before I went my way.

I didn't go far before I found a young mother with two children in the cart, giggling and having fun. She told me that her plan was to have a large family. She said she knew in her heart that God was going to provide. I slipped her a gift card and said "God is providing! Lean on Him, trust Him." There were many tears of joy as we tried to talk.

That was it for this store. I can use these gift cards in other stores as well.

There was a Wendy's nearby still serving breakfast. The parking lot was empty. Seasoned breakfast potatoes (glorified French fries) are yummy! I had $30 on my console ready to give away. I entered the drive-through and ordered the potatoes. "That will be $2.32 please."

I'm thinking, "lots of money left over to give a generous tip!" I offered to pay for the person behind me which was six dollars and change. That left $21 and change. I said to the attendant, "you may have the rest of money if you share it with your coworkers."

She was excited and yelled, "that's awesome. Thank you!" I could see that she quickly called her coworkers and divided the money. As I drove off, I pondered the thought of $30 for a medium specialty type of French fries. Then I chuckled. Her response was priceless! Not bad for the start of the morning.

I proceeded to the chiropractor, who is a believer. I was hoping Dr. Ries could help me get my head on straight. Oh, well, I thought it was funny! We always have godly things to talk about when I am there.

I headed to another grocery store with thoughts of handing out a few more cards. My first instinct was to go past the registers and look for young families to give cards to. The prompting in my spirit was to stay in the produce section. It sounded good to me because I was here for bananas, pineapples, zucchinis, and peppers.

I got what I needed and before I moved on, I heard some kids. I looked up and saw a mother with several children with her, two were seated in the grocery cart. My approach was typical, asking if I could help with defraying the costs of the groceries. She asked inquisitively, "what did you have in mind?" Then I replied, "I'm handing out $50 gift cards to growing families. Are you interested?" "Well, yeah!" We talked for a while, and the kids joined in. Her little girl was excited and wanted to hold the gift card for mom. "It is so awesome what you do. Thank you so much."

During my adventure this morning, two people turned me down, but I did thank them for their honesty. Not everybody wants to receive. I respect their decisions. It is an honor and a joy to be a Christian and give to others.

Luke 6:35, 38

But love your enemies, and do good, and lend, expecting nothing in return, and your reward will be great. Give, and it will be given to you. Good measure, pressed down, shaken together, running over, will be put into your lap. For with the measure you give, it will be measured back to you.

CHAPTER 100
Praying in the aisles

This morning after our men's group, I decided to head to the grocery store in Columbia, since I'm already here in town. Kathleen, the service desk cashier, was glad to see me. I hadn't been there in a while. I purchased five gift cards, then proceeded to hand them out.

Two mothers walked in, each with a cart, and each with a baby. They were friends, shopping together. I watched them, as they were talking and laughing. I approached them and asked if I could bless them each with a gift card. They looked at each other, looked back at me and said, "sure," almost in unison. But they wanted to know why? That led to a great conversation about raising children and the cost of living. After we talked, they thanked me for the cards.

The next three gift cards went to elderly ladies, who were thrilled that somebody would want to help them. Prices seem to skyrocket while living on a fixed income. Not a good scenario. I often wondered how my mother did it, trying to survive on disability income after losing her leg due to diabetes.

I was thinking, "that didn't take long today," as I said goodbye to the cashier. Those were the five gift cards that I purchased here. I do carry extras in case I get in a pinch. As I exited, there was another mother with a baby entering the store. I grabbed a cart for her and told her that this cart comes with a gift card! Smiling and questioning my intentions, she wanted to know why. I answered with, "I just want to be a blessing to families." We had a short but detailed conversation about our purpose in life, growing through trials, and parenting.

Now, in my truck, I was headed home, but I was having too much fun. So, I decided to go to another grocery store and give out some more cards. Little did I know, two divine appointments were waiting for me. The first one is a little different than normal.

As I started through the store, several cashiers noticed that I was there. You should see the smile on their faces when they see me coming. Not that I am anyone special, but it is what I am about, being the hands and feet of Jesus. They know what's about to happen.

I usually look in check-out lines to see if anybody is checking out. I typically ask if they could use some financial help. Today the cashier saw me place a card with someone's food. She knew what to do! She pointed it out to the person checking out. By then I was gone. The story I got later was wonderful. My instincts were correct: the shopper was so grateful for the financial gesture. She asked the cashier how I knew that she could use it? She told her that I don't always know, but it's what I like to do.

By now I had given away four cards. Two of them engaging in great conversation. This often leads to spiritual questions to answer. I talked to one elderly woman for about twenty minutes. I don't get concerned with the time, because that's when God's timing is perfect. Sometimes He will put people in my path to slow me down, so I am at the right place, right time.

Just as I was making my final pass through the store, I was cornered by a gentleman who looked familiar. It was Rick and his wife Susie from Hospice. I had previously given him a $50 card for a large purchase that he made for Hospice. He did not forget it. He told God that the next time he saw me, he wanted to pray for me. Divine appointment? I am here, he is here. We talked briefly, then he asked if he could pray for me. "Absolutely!" There we were, praying in aisle two of the organic section. Wow! What a prayer. You can tell when people have a relationship with God. This man was genuine. He was being the hands and feet of Jesus for me. We talked for another ten minutes about church and ministry. As we shook hands to depart, my next divine appointment arrived. How awesome is God's timing!

Right in front of me was a young mother with her infant. Smiling and cuddling her little one while she was waiting in line. I walked up to her and said, "you are the reason I'm here. I would like to bless you with a $50 gift card." Tears were starting to flow, but the smile remained. After she regained her composure, she said that yesterday her husband was in an auto accident. The truck was totaled, and now they have a rental car. She was grateful for the additional finances.

As I was driving away in my truck, I asked God if there was more that I could've done. I often wish I could do more. I heard nothing, but I felt peace. God will supply their needs as they ask. I guess I was just a spark to kindle the fire.

I still had a little time while I was in town. I stopped by the Mount Joy Food Bank to get an updated list. When I left there, I turned the corner and saw an old man sitting on the porch. As I was passing him, I thought I recognized him. I pulled aside and parked. I got out to talk to him and realized he was my barber from when I was a kid! Charlie has been slowly losing his memory, but he appreciated the time I took for him. He's now 88 years old. When I got home, I wondered, how close to the end was he? I prayed. "Father, if he doesn't know you, please give me the chance to talk to him again, before he enters eternity."

I did get that opportunity to talk to him a few weeks later, but his mind was too confused for much conversation. It was great to spend time with him, despite the circumstances.

2 Peter 3:9-10 NIV

The Lord is not slow in keeping his promise, as some understand slowness. Instead he is patient with you, not wanting anyone to perish, but everyone to come to repentance. But the day of the Lord will come like a thief. The heavens will

disappear with a roar; the elements will be destroyed by fire, and the earth and everything done in it will be laid bare.

CHAPTER 101
The results are in

I asked Raphaela, "the first time we met, what did it mean to you? What were your thoughts by the time you got home? What has changed for you since then?"

"Here is a word of encouragement for you. I was glad to hear that you have a home church. Let your roots grow deep to withstand the storms and let the word of God transform your life."

Raphaela told me: "John, when we first met, I felt profoundly seen. Like through the masks and the humor, I felt like you saw the continuous commitment I had to growth in my communities, in my heart, and in my character. And being seen on a day when the journey was hard, made it feel real."

I don't know what has changed. I think that the times we share and the conversations we have are very important to me. I feel humbled that you share your struggles, because it says that even the strongest need to speak out loud about difficulties. (And that naming things as hard, is not running away from them.)

May I ask why you asked? I didn't tell her that I desired more content for my book. I wanted to show my readers positive results from what I do, to show the kind of impact that can be made when you reach out to people. So, I said it helps me understand my purpose. God placed me in your path for a reason. Sometimes I get to know the reason. Sometimes I don't. I feel a great sense of purpose when I talk to you. I am inspired when I am in your presence. I can't explain it, nor do I have to. There is more to you than meets the eye. It's been a pleasure for me to get to know you.

I started writing my second book. One page I wrote reminds me of you and Richard. You said he is your mentor. I will find it and send it to you.

Here it is: A good mentor is comfortable with your weakness but knowledgeable of your difference. Someone who would pour themselves into you. Judas and John had the same mentor (Jesus). One recognized who he was, the other did not. At times God will hide something that you need in someone you don't enjoy. Everything you wanted is close to you, waiting for your recognition of it.

She replied, "Oh that line about hiding something that you need in someone you don't enjoy is poignant!"

CHAPTER 102
Salt and Light

When Jesus talks about salt and light, He is calling us to holy living.

Is the community blessed by the presence of the church?

Is the church blessed by your presence?

Is your workspace blessed by your presence?

Are your co-workers witnessing your calling?

Do they see your holy living?

Do they see that you are salt and light?

Matthew 5: 13-16 ESV

You are the salt of the earth, but if salt has lost its taste, how shall its saltiness be restored? It is no longer good for anything except to be thrown out and trampled under people's feet. You are the light of the world. A city set on a hill cannot be hidden. Nor do people light a lamp and put it under a basket, but on a stand, and it gives light to all in the house. In the same way, let your light shine before others, so that they may see your good

works and give glory to your Father who is in heaven.

CHAPTER 103
This time I missed the mark

I pulled into the Turkey Hill gas station. Gas was $3.19 a gallon, cheapest place around. They dropped it 40 cents a gallon to create a gas war with the neighboring station. I was almost empty, so I'm going to take advantage of the situation. Little did I know, there was a reason for me to see the price. It got me into a gas station where God wanted me to be. I tell people, eyes open, listen to your surroundings. I had the strong impression that someone needed help with their gasoline purchase. There was a car on the other side of the pump, unoccupied and pre-paying. I saw her come back to the car. Before I had a chance to say anything, she had the nozzle in the tank, filling it. As quickly as she started, she was done! Now thinking to myself, that didn't take long. I hesitated and I blew it!!! She was in her car and gone. I walked around the gas pump and saw that she only put $15 worth in her car. It was less than 5 gallons. I could have helped! I stood before God embarrassed and ashamed.

We all make mistakes, but there is no condemnation.

Romans 8:1 ESV

There is therefore no condemnation for those who are in Christ Jesus.

CHAPTRER 104
Summary

Had it not been for writing this book, *Parkinson's: With Purpose*, and had it not been for Parkinson's, how many stories would not be told, because they would not exist? Had it not been for those who have encouraged me, to have purpose in my pain, where would I be today?

I am doing what others have done for me. In my giving, the people that I've met, the stories that I've heard, the lives that have been changed. A few homeless people can sleep in comfort, some hungry people can sleep after being fed. Some can drive to work because they now have repaired vehicles. One survived a fire that was happening in the bed of his truck. They are all, some form of answered prayer. There are those who now know that they have a purpose and have a reason for living. They have hope and a future. There is a reason to get up in the morning because they know that God has their back.

Would these things have happened if I did not have Parkinson's? There is a reason why God did not remove the thorn from my side. It has helped define who I am as a child of God. It has helped in creating character, by showing me ways to be the hands and feet of Jesus. In the beginning, what I thought was punishment from God was pruning. Although the pruning was painful, it was necessary for bearing fruit. What the enemy meant for harm; God turned into good for His glory. It became the tool for good works. Salvation gets you into heaven, good works are a byproduct. Good works, without salvation, is foolishness. Jesus will say depart from me I never knew you. God didn't make your calling to be easy. He made it so you would have to rely on Him for strength. If you could do it on your own, you would boast. He gave you spiritual gifts to make your calling possible.

Remember that you were created on purpose for a specific purpose. Fulfill the days that God had ordained for you before you were even born.

In 2023, while having Parkinson's, I was used by God to touch over 300 people/families with encouragement, prayers, gift cards, and more.

The ways that you can minister are endless. Find what works for you. Once you enter through the door to eternity, you will never have another opportunity to win one more soul or do good for others. Do it now while you can!

I will attach my email address. Keep me posted on your progress. I have shared my story with others within my church. Now they are doing the same thing: living a fulfilled life despite their personal challenges. You can be perfectly healthy and not know your purpose. You can be extremely ill and discover that you still have purpose.

Once you die, and step through the door to eternity, you can no longer be an answer to somebody's prayer. Your purpose here will be over. Make the most of what you have left. The time is now!

What is your challenge? How do you reach out to people? How do you help people? Hit me up with your story at this email address. I would be honored to take the time to read it.

pdwithpurpose@gmail.com

CHAPTER 105
Nothing more to do!

This book is complete. I laid my pen down.

Like creation:

On the seventh day, God rested. It's not like He was tired from creating the earth and humankind, He rested because He put down His creative tools. There was nothing more He could do to make it better. It was complete, it was finished. Like a painter when he's done with the job. One more stroke of the brush would be too much! The painter put his brush down because his painting was complete.

Genesis 2:1-3 TPT
And so the creation of the heavens and the earth were completed in all their vast array. By the seventh day, God had completed creating his masterpiece, so on the seventh day, he rested from all his work. So God blessed the seventh day and

made it sacred, because on it he paused to rest from all his work of creation.